75 Valorous Stories of Freedom

Dr. Rajendra Patoria

DIAMOND BOOKS

www.diamondbook.in

Publisher : **Diamond Pocket Books (P) Ltd.**
X-30, Okhla Industrial Area, Phase-II
New Delhi-110020
Phone : 011- 40712200
E-mail : wecare@diamondbooks.in
Website : www.diamondbooks.in
Edition : 2025

75 Valorous Stories of Freedom

Author: ***Dr. Rajendra Patoria***
Translator: ***Dr. Nivedita Banerjee***

Prelude

"75 Valorous Stories of Freedom" is the blunt records of the cruelty, atrocity, and inhuman tortures committed by the British Regime. British writers and Journalists themselves have described these heinous crimes in glorious words. They said- "Burning up the Black Hindustanis was a uniquely ecstasic experience for us". Even innocent old women and children were not spared. They were murdered after going through terrible torture. Public hangings, using Elephants for stomping the victims, death by cannon blast, besieging a whole village and then lighting up an inferno to burn people alive, casting victims out in the open sea were the brutal ways of their torture.

The martyrs sent to Andaman for Kalapani punishment suffered hellish agony. The Cellular jail in Port Blair was especially constructed for the purpose. The prison cells were so small that one could not even stretch their legs while lying down. Every cell had doors facing away from the others so that the prisoners could not see each other. Such tortures drove some freedom fighters to self-immolation, and some towards insanity. There were restrictions upon excretions discharged daily, and even for sitting and standing. And all this had to be done in the same cell. They were made to toil like oxen on empty stomachs.

Only because these lakhs of sacrificing souls kept the flame of the struggle burning, we acquired freedom. They knew that their struggle would ultimately culminate into tortures, followed by agonizing death, yet these martyrs forfeit their lives to fuel the altar of freedom.

75 valorous stories of freedom struggle are collected in this book. We should always remember them. It is also necessary to tell the new generation that we did not get freedom without any bloodshed. There was an unbroken tradition of armed resistance to the British rule from its very inception. Soldiers' Mutiny in Bengal, Chuhaad Mutiny, Sanyasi Mutiny, Santhal Mutiny, and other such uprisings ultimately resulted in the first freedom struggle of 1857.

Even after the first freedom struggle, the flame of mutiny was not extinguished. Kuka Revolt in Punjab, Guerilla War by Vasudev Balwantrao in Maharashtra, institutions like Shivaji Samitee and Matridevi Samstha led by Pt. Gendalal Dixit in United Province (U.P.), kept the flame of the struggle alive. Rash Behari Bose and Sachindra Nath Sanyal from Bengal inculcated the aspiration of freedom in the soldiers of Bengal, Bihar, Delhi, Rajasthan, United Province, and Punjab by infiletrating the Soldiers' Camps and prepared them for the revolt of 1915, but unfortunately the Mission failed. Raja Mahendrapratap even established an Interim Indian Govternment in Afghanistan and fought with the British India.

Rash Behari Bose created favorable conditions in Japan for Azad Hind Fauj and handed its reins to Subhash Chandra Bose. This army unfurled its flag on the Indian soil. The movement received hearty welcome in India. The British were running their government with a handful of their military and masses of Indian soldiers. By the efforts of Subhash Babu, Indian masses and the Indian soldiers under British Army were awakened towards freedom movement.

Armed revolutionaries did not get proper co-operation and sympathy from the public in their early days. Their institutions were mostly secret. Their revolt was based on the idea of involving minimum people and maximizing their sacrifice. These revolts laid the foundation to our independence.

The tales of sacrifices by these martyrs are vanishing with the passage of time. Our sincere wish is that their stories get etched in the mind of every Indian. And the new generation should acknowledge and remember them. We know that there are many more stories whose memories are now lost. But the ones that are not need to be preserved, and be told to the new generation.

The efforts of these revolutionaries were significant in freeing India from the bonds of slavery. Their struggles brought us freedom but many of them had to live the degrading life of unacknowledged anonymity. It is my conviction that the Amrit Mahotsav of India's independence is an opportune time for this book to be of immense value to everyone.

–Dr. Rajendra Patoria
Azad Chowk, Sadar Bazar, Nagpur- 400001
Phone- 0712-2520327, Mob. No.- 9421779906

Contents

The sacrifice of three brothers

Damodar Hari Chapekar, Balkrishna Hari Chapekar, and Vasudev Chapekar were Chittpawan Brahmins, living in Pune.

At the time, Lokmanya Tilak's speeches were invoking national consciousness in Maharashtra and these three brothers, especially the eldest, Shri Damodar Hari Chapekar, were devotees of Lokmanya Tilak.

Since childhood, Damodar Chapekar was interested in physical exercises and wielding weapons. He aimed to join the Army so as to provoke the Indian soldiers to revolt, after finishing formal education. Even after two attempts, he was denied the opportunity because the government was well aware of his intentions and movements.

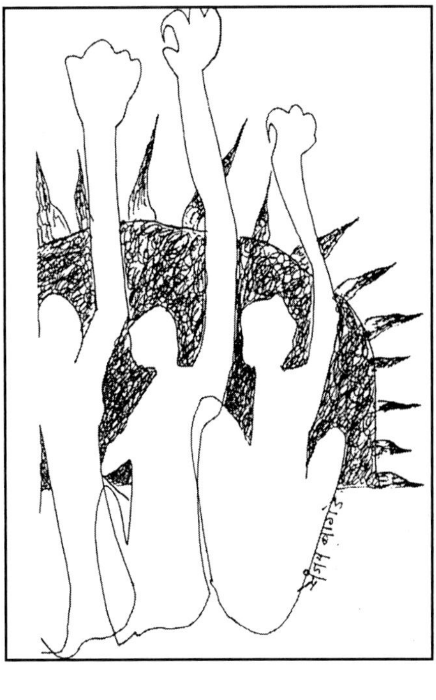

So what, if he could not join the Army! Damodar himself created an Army by gathering young men in which he himself gave Army training to the joinees. This youth Army took upon itself to liberate the country and some audacities committed by Damodar Chapekar individually made the government wary of him.

What is the relevance of Queen Victoria's statue in India? Damodar Chapekar smeared tar on the statue of Queen Victoria in Mumbai and garlanded it with shoes. In Mumbai again, he burnt the giant *pandal* which was prepared for holding Matric Examination because the epidemic of Cholera was spread in Mumbai at that time and its natives were opposing the examination while the government ignored their concerns. Even in Pune, Damodar Chapekar burnt the *pandal* which was made for catering to the entertainment government officials. Despite such deeds, the government remained clueless about the perpetrator. Damodar was destined to do something even bigger, how could he be ensnared yet?

In 1897, the Chapekar trio were dwelling in Pune when the epidemic of Plague epidemic had spread acutely. Most of the households were ruined by the plague. Those spared, were destroyed by the Plague Commissioner Mr. Rand and his colleagues. The government officials, under the pretext of vacating the houses would enter houses, confistcate the valuables and throw out the rest of its contents. They would forcefully drag the people from their houses and even made it a point to assault the women in the process. They burnt many houses by proclaiming that the house was too contaminated to remain standing.

When Punekars were suffering under the atrocities of Rand, Lokmanya Tilak wrote rebellious articles in newspapers against him. Damodar Chapekar decided to uproot the problem at its source. In this mission, his younger brother Balkrishna Chapekar and his friend Mahadev Vinayak Ranadey were his companions. They planned to exterminate Rand on 22nd June 1897 during

Queen Victoria's jubilee celebrations. They decided to gift Rand with death. They wrote a letter to Rand with a message that 'the day of Queen Victoria's jubilee celebration will be his last day'. Intoxicated with the power of British rule, Rand just ignored the paper-threat. He believed that all Indians tremble in fear upon seeing an Englishman so they can never attempt such feat.

At last, the fateful day of 22nd June arrived when the Diamond Jubilee function of Queen Victoria was to be celebrated in Pune. Chapekar woke up in morning and prayed to God for success. He was recalling the story of Arjun in which he vowed to kill Jaidrath before sunset. Even they had the limited time of up to 12 o'clock midnight to fulfill their vow. The Chapekar *Bandhu* practiced identifying Rand in advance because they wanted to kill only him to fulfill their challenge and no one else. Many a times Damodar Chapekar snooped upon Rand, pretending to enquire his coachman about jobs, he enquired about Rand. To get the exact location of Rand's house he also enquired the Postman of that area. His younger brother Vasudev minutely observed Rand's routine and habits.

On 22nd June 1897, the revolutionaries were fully active. In the afternoon, they went to the Government House to search for him but could not figure out Rand's location. Afterwards, they went to St. Mary's Church where Rand was present but they could not make any move because of the crowd and they went back, despodent.

The revolutionaries knew about the function at Government House to be held in the evening, so they went there again in the evening, at exactly 7:30 PM. Rand also arrived there but because of many other carts near Rand's cart that the revolutionaries could not fulfill their objective. They got worried because the only chance they will now get to kill Rand was when he returns from the function, or else their vows will be ruined.

Everyone was prepared with his weapon. Pistols tucked in their waists, swords were tied with rags of *Pagdi* from their waist till thigh. Thus they waited for Rand. They were getting restless with the passage of time. The celebrations continued till 11:30 p.m. that night while they carried on with their *morchabandi.* Damodar Chapekar was at the gate of the Government House. His younger brother Balkrishna was stationed a bit farther, followed by Ranadey. Planning was to ensure that if one of them fails the other two can get Rand and will not miss to kill him. If the pistols did not work, they will strike with their swords so that the vow could be fulfilled.

At 11:30, Rand's cart started rolling. Damodar Chapekar followed the cart. He planned that once the cart separates from the crowd, he would aim to kill Rand. At a distance, there was another cart carrying another Englishman Mr. Ayerst and his wife. Damodar followed Rand's cart by running fast so that he could mentain minimum distance between him and the cart. As soon as the cart reached to Pili Kothi of Jamshedji, Balkrishna Chapekar shouted, *'Naarya*! *Naarya*!', to signal others. Rand heard it too but dismissed it as some villager calling out to his friends. Upon receiving the signal, Damodar Chapekar swiftly reached Rand's cart and leapt on its back-step. He pulled the curtain off the cart's door, reached inside the cart with his pistol and pulled the trigger. Rand fell down inside the cart. Mr. Ayerst cart was at a short distance from Rand's. Although he as drunk, his wife saw a robust man leaping and running away from the back-step of Rand's cart. She was in the midst of narrating this to her husband when suddenly there was an explosion, a bullet struck him and he fell on her lap. The revolutionaries had fled from the spot and could not be traced even after many searches. Mr. Ayerst died immediately while Rand died on 3rd July 1897. The search for the murderers gained even more momemtum.

After 2 months of Rand's death, Damodar Chapekar was caught. After a few days, Balkrishna Chapekar was also caught. They both were prosecuted. Damodar Chapekar was sentenced to Death by Hanging and 18th April 1898 was the date fixed for his Hanging.

Damodar Chapekar must have slept peacefully that night before he was to be hanged in the morning. He woke up in the morning, prayed to the God, and got ready for the hanging. As his last wish, he held *Geeta Rahasya* written by Lokmanya Tilak in his hand. The appointed time for hanging had arrived but the magistrate did not reach there on time. Damodar Chapekar was getting restless to be rewarded with death for loving his country. He sarcastically commented upon the time management of the British. Finally, when the magistrate arrived and gave the order, Damodar Chapekar stood on the gallows with a smile on his face and *Gita Rahasya* in his hand. The executioner tied the noose on his neck and removed the scaffold beneath. Damodar Chapekar's body hung on the noose. Even in death's grip, his hand kept holding the *Gita Rahasya*. The book remained his companion in his pyre.

So, on 18th April 1898, at 6:40 a.m., the brave patriot left the lap of his beloved motherland for the heavenly abode.

The youngest brother Vasudev Chapekar was very miserable. He felt that his brothers received the prize for their patriotism by being sentenced to death, and he was left alone. He went to his mother and told her, "Ma! my both the brothers are now in the lap of God, I too want to sacrifice his life to the God as well."

What could his mother reply to him? With tears in her eyes, she kissed her son.

Vasudev took the vow to take revenge from the Dravid Bandhus who helped the police in catching his brothers. Disguised as a Punjabi, he went to their house at night and told them that the Constable has asked them to come to the police station for an important questioning. They were playing cards and told him to leave while they will follow later. Vasudev hid near a well and waited for Dravid Bandhus to leave for the police station. As soon as Dravid Bandhus reached near, he fired at them. Both the traitors died on the spot. They had betrayed the Chapekars for the prize money of 20000 Rupees. Vasudev gave them the prize of bullets.

For many days, nobody was caught for the crime. Ultimately, because innocent persons were being harassed, Vasudev Chapekar surrendered himself before the police and confessed. Ranade had been caught earlier. Cases were filed against both of them and they both were given death penalty.

On the morning of 8th May 1899 when Vasudev Chapekar was being taken to the gallows, he came across the cell in which is elder brother, Balkrishna Chapekar, was imprisoned. Vasudev shouted- "goodbye brother, I am going."

Balkrishna Chapekar's voice came from the cell, "Alright! Good bye. I will meet you both, soon,"

The brothers finally met. Vasudev was hanged on 8th May while Balakrishna was hanged on 12th May 1899.

And thus, the three Chapekar Bandhus kissed the hanging noose with smile on their faces (1897).

★★★

Son! Be brave at the time of hanging

The Convocation ceremony of Punjab University of 23rd December 1930 was headed by Governor Geoffrey Fitzhervey de Montmorency. The Convocation address was given by Dr. Sarvepalli Radhakrishnan who was dressed up in a suit and wore polished shoes. Harikishan had arrived before time. He had a dictionary with him in which he had hidden a revolver by cutting out the middle portion of its pages. As soon as the function was over and the crowd started disbursing, Harikishan stood up on a chair and fired a bullet towards the Governor, which scratched his arm. He fired a second shot which grazed the back of the Governor. He wanted to fire the gun for the third time but Dr. Radhakrishnan stood in between, to save the Governor. Harkishan could not fire. He ran out of the hall and reached the porch. The Police chased him. Police inspector Chanan Singh jumped towards him. Harikishan warned him to stop but he did not. At last, Harkishan fired a bullet and Chanan Singh fell down. One more policeman ran towards him and Harkishan shot him too, but he managed to survive by laying himself down on the ground. All Harkishan's bullets were spent. He wanted to reload the gun but was overpowered and caught.

After getting caught, Harkishan was beaten severely. His clothes were stripped off and he was made to lie on a bar of ice while one more bar was put on top of his body. This happened during the winter season. He was trapped with ice bars both above and beneath his body. Every day he went through this hellish torture.

On 2nd January 1930, the primary investigation started and he was handed over to the Session Court where he declared- "The thousands of countrymen who are struggling for the freedom of this country, men, women, and young ones who are in jail have faced abuse and severe beatings. Hence, I have lost my faith in non-violence and now believe in armed revolution.

Churchill's speech has assured me that the English people will never let India be free. So, I resolved to do something. I hold the Governor responsible for this grueling oppression. I purchased a revolver for Rs.95/- and decided to punish the Governor at the convocation ceremony because there would have many eminent people to witness his punishment".

On 26th January 1931, the Lahore Session Judge declared death sentence for Harkishan. The High Court also sustained that judgment. When he met his grandmother in jail, she told him, "son, be brave at the time of hanging".

When his father went to the Lahore jail to meet his eldest son, Harkishan, who was eager to kiss the hanging noose, he did not ask anything regarding his health. He did not even ask if Harkishan was comfortable in the jail. In Pashto language, he asked, "Son! I have trained you to be a good marksman and you never failed to hit the target. Then how come you fired two bullets at the Governor and he still survived?"

Harkishan said with honesty, "I intended to fire the third bullet but Dr. Radhakrishnan stood in front of the Governor to save him, so I couldn't fire the third bullet".

Father said, "If you had hit your target and the Governor had been killed, I would have been extremely proud of you".

★★★

Viceroy's Procession; a flopped show

On 23rd December 1912, the convoy of Viceroy Lord Hardinge arrived in Delhi like a grand gala. Instead of Kolkata, he had chosen Delhi as the capital of India so he wanted to enter the city with pomp and splendour. The presence of all the Rajas,

Maharajas, and Princes was adding colour to the opulance. Millions of people from the nearby cities and villages had arrived to watch the *Juloos* and they crowded the roadside, hung from rooftops, windows, and galleries.

In front of the Majestic *juloos,* a decorated band of soldiers was playing music. Behind the band, soldiers with guns were marching, followed by armed soldiers on horses. A giant decorated elephant was moving behind them carrying the Viceroy in a grand *hauda*. On the elephant, the *mahawat* was sitting at the front followed by Viceroy's Guard, Colonel Maxwell. Then there was Viceroy's wife and the Viceroy in the *Hauda*. *Jamadar* Mahavir Singh of Balrampur sat at the very rear on the elephant, carrying the umbrella for the Viceroy.

As soon as the *Juloos* reached at the center of Chandni Chowk, near Ghantaghar, right in front of Punjab National Bank, there was a sudden loud explosion with a flash of light. The sound was that of an exploding bomb that was thrown upon the Viceroy from a nearby building. The *Juloos* stopped abruptly. No one understood what had happened. But when they saw the *Jamadar* hanging arkwardly from the elephant, people came to understand that he was rendered lifeless due to the blast of the bomb. It was Viceroy's good

fortune that the bomb did not strike him. The back seat of the *hauda* was totally smashed and splinters of wood made a four inch cut on Viceroy's back and his shoulder bone was badly injured. He also received some minor cuts on his body. Those who were sitting in the front, his wife, Colonel Maxwell and the *Mahavat* were safe but they did go deaf for a while due to the explosion. The Viceroy regained his senses after some time, but ultimately collapsed on the *hauda*. He was carried away from the elephant and the police started *nakabandi*. Because of the explosion, people started to scream and shout and run *helter-skelter* in order to find safety for themselves. People who were on the rooftops came down and ran as well.

Vasant Kumar Vishwas was the person who threw the bomb at the Viceroy. Vasant Kumar was a young, slim, short heighted, and fair looking boy who was disguised as a girl wearing ornaments. He mingled with the ladies who were watching the *Juloos* from the rooftop of Punjab National Bank. He was sitting behind the ladies and, therefore, got the chance to throw the bomb unnoticed. Bomb was made inside a cigarette box. It was quite small and thus Vasant Kumar had no problem hiding it in the *saree* he wore. On the footpath, under the same building, Rash Behari Bose was pretending to watch the *Juloos* disguised as a *Seth*. After the blast, the faux girl, Vasant Kumar, descended from the rooftop and joined her guardian *Seth*, only to disappear within the mob.

Although Rash Behari Bose failed to kill the Viceroy, this explosion spread waves of panic both within the country and outside. This explosion was pivotal in scaring the British rulers and bringing a change their policies towards Indians.

★★★

Broke the Police Corden

Savarkar was arrested in England on the basis of a warrant issued in Bombay, now Mumbai. So as to carry him back to Mumbai, he was made to board a ship named Moriya along with the police. On the ship, he was surrounded by the British soldiers carrying heavy ammunition. Iyer and his companion came to the port to bid farewell to Savarkar. Savarkar knew that if his case is opened in the court, he would receive a death sentence or, at least, *Kala Pani* for life.

He decided to free himself from the clutches of the British soldiers, by any means, before reaching Mumbai.

So he told Iyer in Hindi that they should reach Marseille port earlier because he had decided to leave the ship mid-way.

Although Savarkar spoke to Iyer in Hindi, the British soldiers suspected something. They doubled up their surveillance. The ship sailed. When the ship was near the French port Marseille, Savarkar asked the British soldiers to take him to the toilet. Soldiers waited outside, closed the door and locked it from the inside. There was a big mirror in the toilet, which showed the view inside to those outside. He covered the mirror with a cloth. There was a ventilator in the toilet which was like a small hole but a smart man could trick his way out of it. After trying twice or thrice, Savarkar was successful in wriggling out of the ventilator and jumped into the sea.

The sound of his sea dive alerted the soldiers. They saw that Savarkar was swimming rapidly towards Marseille port. British soldiers chased him on their boats and shot at him. Savarkar somehow made it to the Port by dodging the bullets. He started running in search of a French policeman, as soon as he touched France.

British soldiers started shouting 'Thief! Thief!' to mislead, as they ran after Savarkar. At last, Savarkar found a French policeman. He told him that he was not a thief but a political prisoner and asked them to take him to a Police Station as British soldiers could not arrest him in France. However, the French Policeman could not understand his language and handed him over to the British police in lieu of a bribe. Savarkar was imprisoned again.

A British policeman assaulted him with a punch. In retaliation, Savarkar also gave him such a tight slap that he fell down, became unconscious. But this resulted in handcuffs for Savarkar. Savarkar was disappointed that his friends, Iyer and others could not reach the port in time. Iyer, Madam Cama, and others had reached the port after Savarkar got rearrested.

Savarkar was boarded into the ship again and kept under strict surveillance. On 7th July 1911 Savarkar disembarked on his motherland as a prisoner with armed soldiers as his welcome band. He was then carried to Nashik in an enclosed vehicle and jailed. (1911)

★★★

Unique planning of 150 women for Jouhar

Shocked by British defeat at the hands of Amar Singh, Brigadier Douglas and General Lugard became determined to finish him off. Amar Singh had a very small army while the British had a big armed force with them. Amar Singh divided his army in small groups and spread them strategically. His Revolutionary Army was concealed at multiple locations. When the Revolutionary Army created a ruckus somewhere, the British would rush in with their forces to suppress them, leaving behind an empty ground to be captured by another group of the Revolutionary Army. Thus, the British Army kept being deceived and defeated, repeatedly. Frustrated, General Lugard took retirement and went back to England.

When Amar Singh left Jagdishpur to attack Aara, the British Army engulfed Jagdishpur to prevent his return. However, Amar Singh bamboozled the British Army, again. He spread rumours through his spys that he had reached Aara and captured it. While the British Army was marching towards Aara, Amar Singh returned to Jagdishpur.

This kind of cunning drove the British crazy. Brigadier Douglas swore to kill Amar Singh in shortly. He declared hefty rewards for killing Amar Singh. Moreover, he took 7000 soldiers who completely surrounded Jagdishpur. He divided the soldiers in 7 groups and proceeded towards Jagdishpur. He established *chowkies* at different places so that no one could escape out of Jagdishpur. He thought that he had imprisoned the Lion in a cage and he would kill him inside the cage only.

Amar Singh came to know about this, he vowed to escape unscathed. When the British Army started attacking on Jagdishpur, 6 groups arrived on time from six different directions. The seventh group, however, was a bit delayed and lost its contact with the other groups of soldiers. Amar Singh took advantage of the delay and escaped from the direction from where the seventh group was supposed to attack. Brigadier Douglas lost not only the opportunity but also his face.

The British Army came back to encircle the revolutionaries with more strength and vigour. Out of 400 revolutionaries, 300 died. The rest hundred revolutionaries dispersed themselves randomly in the arena and each started attacking the British soldiers with the wild ferocity of a lion. In the end, only three revolutionaries were left standing. Amar Singh was one of them. They plowed their way through the enemy and escaped. British soldiers had once managed to locate Amar Singh on the back of an elephant. By the time they could circle the Elephant, Amar Singh had jumped down and was lost in the melee of fighters. These revolutionaries faught valiantly in every nook and cranny of their homeland but neither surrendered, nor ever accepted defeat. Their fighting spirits have created glorious records of bravery, art of war, and love for freedom. Nobody knows where Amar Singh eloped or how he died.

As the war ended, 150 women set a unique example of *Jauhar* in the *Ranivaas* of Jagdishpur. Each lined-up herself in front of a cannon and, with her own hands, lit a string that fired the cannon. Thus, 150 women blew themselves up to smithereens rather than surrender to the enemy.

★★★

Chewed by hunting dogs

He was the Bhamashah of his time who had the ardent longing for his country's freedom in his heart. He not only had the immense wealth to fuel the freedom struggle movement but also had the fertile mind that could conjure plans for creating spy network and war strategies. His name was Jagat Singh Ramji Das Gurwala.

Seth Ramji Das Gurwala was one of the most respected dignitaries in the court of the last Mughal Emperor of Bahadur Shah Zafar. He was bestowed with many titles and was offered a special seat the emperor's court. Special soldiers were also deputed at his Palace. The Diwali celebrations carried at his home were always attended by the Mughal Emperor himself, in which Seth Sahab used to gift the Emperor 2 lakh *Ashrafies*.

This was the time when in Mughal court was full of selfish members who were engaged in debauchery and hedonistic pursuits. They themselves wanted the empire to collapse so that they get the chance to establish themselves.

Seth Ramji Das provided crores of Rupees to Badshah Bahadur Shah Zafar to build an Integrated Army that would have the strength and mettle to oppose the British. The department of Espionage was developed by the Seth himself that kept an eye on the British and well as the traitorous countrymen.

Seth Ramji Das Gurwala had provided crores of Rupees as help, and billions as loan to Bahadur Shah Zafar to fecilitate the success of Mutiny of 1857. On top of that, his grainery was always open to provide food for the soldiers.

Even the British acknowledged his influence and sought his help but were denied.

When British gained power, one of the first things they did was to set Hunting Dogs lose upon Seth Ramji Das Gurwala, publically, in Delhi's Chandni Chowk. The dogs lacerated and mutilated his body, which the British then displayed in public hanging.

★★★

Exercise before hanging

During his stay in jail, Rajendra Nath Lahiri had two indulgences, one was exercising and the other was reading books. In the arena, he wrestled with Thakur Roshan Singh. Although many of the inmates indulged in books but Rajendra Nath Lahiri was a better reader than anyone else.

On 6th April 1927, the decision on *Kakori Kaand* was declared. Everybody knew what the decision would be. All revolutionaries were sure that Ram Prasad Bismil and Rajendra Nath Lahiri would be awarded Death Sentence. Rajendra Nath Lahiri himself was so sure about it that even after the declaration of his death sentence he was his usual self, as if nothing new had happened. He bore the same sweet smile on his face. After the judgement he said, "I have few days of trouble, it will end after one or two months but I am worried about those who have to remain in jail for 14 to 20 years."

On 17th December 1927, Rajendra woke up as usual and did his physical exercises. He used to do 500 sit-ups everyday. He did same on that day. After bathing he also offered prayer to the God. Then he went happily with the jailer who narrated the whole affair to the British judge. The British judge asked Rajendra, "You offered your prayer to the God, which I can understand. It can be done anytime, especially when it is your last day of life. But I don't understand why you did your physical exercise?"

Rajendra Nath Lahiri replied innocently, "Judge Sir, exercise is my daily routine. I never failed in doing it. Then on the last day of my life, due to fear of death, why should I fail? There is one more reason for my exercise. We Hindus believe in rebirth. I did it because I want to die with strong body, so when I get my next birth I will come back with a strong body to fight with the British Empire again."

This kind of reply from a prisoner, who had only a few minutes of life left to him, stunned the judge.

Standing on the gallows, Rajendra shouted, *"Bharat mata ki Jay! Vande Mataram!"*

★★★

The first Freedom War by farmers and hermits

Patna was the centre of the first farmer upheaval and Sanyasi revolution. Revolutionary farmers united to make an army and stopped the revenue collection by the East India Company. The Rebel Army fought near Patna in and occupied the Husepur Fort which was previously occupied by the British. But after sometime, the Company's Army defeated the rebels and got hold of the fort again. In the mean time, in the jungle area of Bengal, a large number of hermits assembled

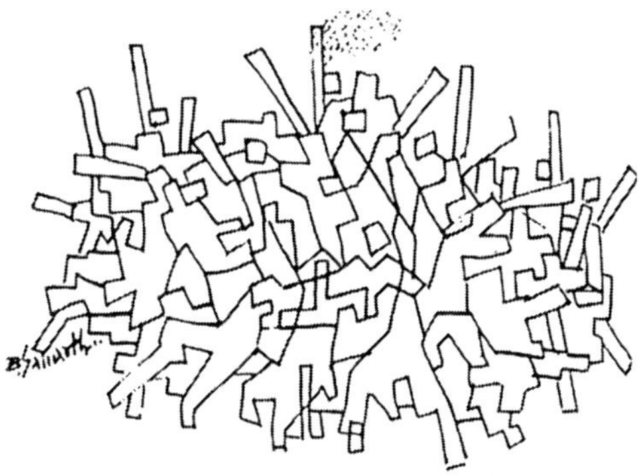

and vowed to struggle against Company's rule. In Jalpaiguri District, they had made an organized Fort. The British Army, led by captain Macheji went there to suppress the revolution but failed twice. In 1770, Macheji coaxed and coerced the local people to help him enter the forest area. Meanwhile, the rebels had moved towards north to prepare for the next war. The British Army mistook it to be their victory.

In the winter, the revolutionaries attacked the British Army and drove them further to Rangpur. At the same time, Lieutenant Kaith was killed in an attack in Morang area, near the Nepal border. The British Army was scattered and its Hindustani soldiers joined the rebels.

In 1771, the rebel soldiers subjugated the British Army and attacked Purnea district. They organised huge army in Dinajpur with the help of revolutionaries from Rangpur and Mymensingh.

In February 1771, the rebels started looting the bungalows and offices of British people, along with those of the Indian land-lords and businessmen who supported the British. Some of the Sanyasi leaders wandered through different villages to unite the local farmers and traditional workers and inspired them to fight for freedom from the Company Raj. Approximately two and half thousand rebel soldiers fought the British Army near Pondvardhan, under the leadership of Majnu Shah Fakir. Although the British won the war but Lieutenant Fentaham died. After the defeat, Majnu Shah and his followers took shelter in the old Fort of Mahasthan and proceeded towards Bihar. Majnu Shah took up the mission to bring awareness amongst the masses and prepare them for military struggle against the British. Consequently in many villages like Silberi, in Bogura district, the revolutionaries disrupted the lives of the British people. The Court of the Company and its Business Centre in Nur Nagar were looted. Owing to this success, the local farmers joined with revolutionaries and started helping Fakirs and Saints who were rebel leaders in disguise.

By 1773, Rangpur had become the centre of Sanyasi revolt. British Army's leader, Captain Thomas, attacked Rangpur with a huge army but to avoid bringing the general public into the battle, the revolutionaries lured the enemy soldiers by running far into the forest. The British Army took this as a victory. They thought that the rebel Sanyasis deserted the place without fight. They started victory celebrations by lighting up their bombs, ammunitions, and whatever they had for war. But revolutionaries and Farmers' Army together attacked the British Army, out of the blue. Even the Hindustani soldiers of British Army revolted. The British ran and escaped to the forest where the farmers searched and killed them. In this struggle, Captain Thomas died. But in March 1773 when Sanyasi rebels were celebrating victory of killing Captain Edwards and defeating his army, the British Army overpowered them. They arrested maximum number of rebels and hanged them.

The Governor General Hestings had released strict orders to suppress the revolt. He also ordered that people should not give shelter to the revolutionaries. People should inform the British about them and if anybody is found to be protecting them they may face even Death Sentence. Due to these Orders many innocent villagers were hanged. The British imposed false allegations on many to be a protector of revolutionaries or being a rebel themselves.

From 1774 to 1775, Majnu Shah tried to organise the rebel hermits of Bihar and Bengal. On 15th November 1776, the Sanyasi revolutionaries had made a camp to rest. The British Army stealthly invaded their camp and revolutionaries were forced to move back. The British Army chased them. As they reached near the forest, the revolutionaries started attacking back. Many British soldiers died and their leader Lieutenant Robertson became an invalid. Majnu Shah and his followers ran away.

To organise the army, Majnu Shah took revenue from the landlords of Bihar and Bengal. On 27th December 1786 Majnu Shah was injured badly during a war with British Army and after 2 days the chief leader of the Sanyasi mutiny sacrificed his life.

After the death of Majnu Shah, the rebellion continued under the leadership of his brother Musa Shah, although it had lost much of its force. Two ardent followers of Majnu Shah, Gul Shahar and Chirag Ali, were also a part of the group. After sometime due to internal disputes, Gul Shahar killed Musa Shah.

From June 1877, this movement was carried by the famous leader Bhavani Pathak and Devi Chaudhurani. They had disrupted fights with the British Army. A huge army of British once surrounded Bhavani Pathak in a Naval war and ultimately Bhavani Pathak and his followers died. Devi Chaudhurani took the lead of the revolution from there on but history is not very clear about how it ends from here on.

★★★

Organised a Group of Courtesans

One of the famous and memorable characters involved in 1857's first battle for freedom is that of Ajijan, a courtesan from Kanpur. There were many courtesans who devoted their life to the pyre of freedom. British historian, T.R. Homes has acknowledged the role of these ladies in the revolt in 1857. The British soldiers in Meerut went to their infamous establishments to seek sensual pleasures but they were disdained by these women and had their manhood was challenged. They used to say, "Your brothers have been handcuffed for opposing slavery but you men are getting high on debauchery. To hell with you! You should wear bangles in your hands."

T.R. Homes speculated that riled up by the taunts of the courtesans, the soldiers returnd to their cantonment and lit up explosion to drown the frustration they carried from Meerut's Pari Bazar. Ajijan was a prominent spark in this episode.

During the insurgence, the rebels used to take shelter in the abodes of Subedar Tika Singh and Shamsuddin Khan. Ajijan was madly in love with Shamsuddin Khan. So she was also a participant in the conspiracies and plannings of rebels. On 22nd May 1857, Nana Sahib Peshwa entered Kanpur with 300 bodyguards, 2 elephants, 3 cannons, and thousands of soldiers. Subedar Tika Singh, Jwala Prasad, and Shamsuddin Khan were trusted by Nana Sahib. District collector Hilsirdon had given the responsibility of protecting the treasury to Nana Sahib Peshwa. However, he was thinking about capturing the treasury to build a bigger army. His aim was to destroy the British and free the country.

At last, on June 1, 1857 in consultation with Azimullah, Tika Singh, Shamsuddin, and Tatya Tope, Nana Saheb resolved to start the war for freedom war from Kanpur. Sitting on a boat in the middle of river Ganga, Nana Saheb scooped up the holy waters in his palm and took the oath to initiate the war for freedom. Ajijan distributed sweets when this news reached her. She informed Nana Saheb that she would also act as a soldier in this war.

On June 4, 1857, Tika Singh led the rebellion of *Jang-e-Aazaadi*. Along with the soldiers riding with swords in their hands was Ajijan holding the rebel flag. The troops saluted Tika Singh and started looting the government treasury. Within no time, Tatya Tope held the keys to the treasury. Armaments and money were distributed amongst the rebels and thus started the Gorilla Warfare in Kanpur. The British were weakening against the rebels. When on June 7, 1857 rebles captured the Seat of Kanpur, Ajijan was seen distributing sweets and *Sharbat* to the battle-worn soldiers. Her sword, slung by her side, was smattered with the blood of two British soldiers whom she had killed in the battle.

The flags of East India Company were stripped off various government buildings were set on fire. Nana Saheb Peshwa declared himself as Head of Kanpur. Tatya Tope was made the Commander of theArmy, and Tika Singh was conferred with the leadership of the Equsterian Troops. Shamsuddin was awarded

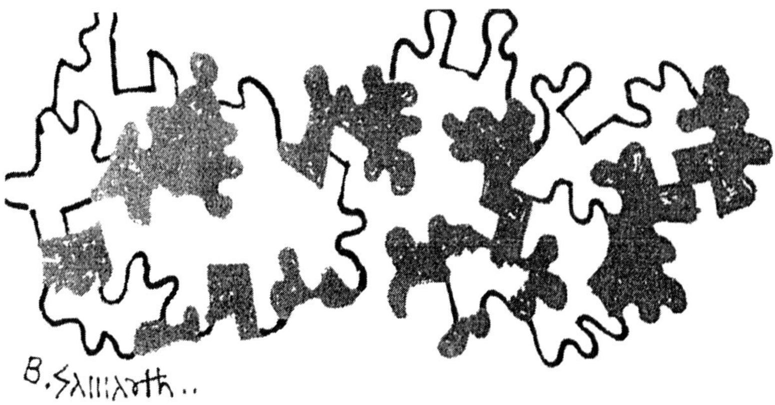

ministership. It was one of the best moments of Ajijan's life. In a way, she secretly held the powers of Kanpur in her grasp. Nana Saheb made her his advisor.

Ajijan seduced the British Officers to divulge their secrets to her and pass on the information to rebels. She organised about 400 prostitutes and built the *Mastani Toli*. They all were involved in the work of providing food items and ammunitions to Indian soldiers. She also killed many British officers.

The British attacked back on Kanpur with the help of General Havelock. This time, the British soldiers were fully prepared. A big battle was fought in Kanpur. The rebels were overwhelmed. Most of them were captured and hanged by the trees. Nana Saheb Peshwa and Tatya Tope disappeared underground.

Ajijan was also imprisoned. She was young and beautiful and thus the British were willing to pardon her if she confessed to her alleged crimes. Proud Ajijan did not accept the proposal. She was hanged. She had fulfilled her duty towards her motherland.

★★★

Heap of corpses at Jallianwala Bagh

13th April 1919, Sunday, near Swarna Mandir, it was around 4:30 p.m. at Jallianwala Bagh... The British Army marched with the euqesterian troops at the front, followed by General Dyer in the car. Cannons and armored vehicles; Scraping of boots of the soldiers marching; the armed platoon of British Army! The sound of their steady march and halt! It was a scene at the time of Baisakhi, people assembled in Jallianwala Bagh.

The English Army divided in two troops entered the Bagh and encircled the crowd inside, and loaded their rifles. Although, they had machine guns, the gate was too small; machine guns had to be kept outside but loaded. The public in the Bagh were surrounded by the English Army from inside and outside.

In the meeting, suddenly there were whispers to see the Army. They were meeting to enjoy Baisakhi, the main festival of Punjab. Without any warning General Dyre ordered to fire.

Getting the order, all rifles turned towards the peoples and the bullets of 303 rifels started shooting extravagantly. Rudely and unreasonably 20,000 people had been attacked in this meeting. Thousands of people were killed and many injured. The soil of Jallianwala Bagh was drenched with blood. Many of them tried to escape but there was no way. There was no place to hide. The ground was filled with shrill cry. This has been the most heinous crime done by the British government , which will be remembered in history. Aeroplanes were hovering making fearful noise. These were the images of British in human cruelity and atrocity.

The ground of Jallianwala Bagh was situated within 8 acres of land, which was surrounded by big palaces and buildings. There was only one broad opening of 8 feet on which British soldiers were deployed. There was no other escape route. Bullets were also coming from outside. Without any hindrance, theArmy was firing bullets from every direction. Thousands of people, young, old, women & children were stucked inside.

The man who was addressing the meeting was shouting "Calm down please. Britishers won't fire on unarmed persons. Don't panic, these are blank fires." But with the continuous firing, the people were falling and dying, everywhere the strains of blood, everyone shouting for help. What example one can put before this sort of traumatizing incident!

People were in dilemma how to save life. They were not alert for this attack rather they were attacked suddenly and mercilessly.

The main aim of General Dyre was to kill people; that's why he came with army troop silently. He did not give a chance to think or act to the innocent people. General Dyre was mad with cruelity; and he had discussed and planned the attack with his colleagues because he thought that he was not attacking people but enemies.

General ordered not to fire in air but on people. Army did the same and killed so many persons. The bullets were raining, one after another and the devastation was incomprehensible. Some people lie down on the ground but could not escape bullets. The people were searching another way to run but there were so narrow ways and due to huge mob, when everybody tried to escape, the pushing and crowding made them more unsafe. General ordered to fire on the mob.

People were killed at once and there was a heap of corpses. People tried to escape even by jumping the wall but Dyre indicated towards those spots and they were also killed. Some of them were stumped, some were crushed, some had bullets, and there was a chaos on the ground. Every moment, the number of corpses was increasing. Many persons jumped into a well situated at the centre of ground. Even then they could not save themselves. The ground filled with the sound of distress and uproar. The whole atmosphere was full of shouting and crying.

According to Motilal Committee report, the total number of dead was approximately 1500, whereas Britishers said it was only 450 men, 50 children and 1000 people were injured. Shooting lasted for 15 minutes. Approximately 2000 rounds of bullets were shot at. General Dyre ordered the Army to march back. He did not bother about the dead bodies or injured people. As if it was not his duty. Curfew was imposed. Even relatives were not allowed to search for their own people. Such was the atrocity.

★★★

She was Durga indeed

Enemy entered the Fort through open door. Jhalkari Bai, the commander of Durga dal, was worried for the safety of Rani Lakshmi Bai. She was fighting with Britishers and was thinking of the ways to protect their queen. Golandaj Puran Bahadur died in war for his duty and country. Jhalkari was numb for some time after getting the news. But immediately, she resumed her role. It was not the time to be sad for the separation from her beloved. This was the time to do the duty. Her responsibility became double. She forgot about her husband's death and thought that true homage to her husband was to follow his principles. It was the time to save the Queen's honour. Enemy has entered the fort and sound of distress was everywhere.

Any how Jhalkari reached Queen's palace. After giving her complete information she planned the escape route for Queen and her step son. Jhalkari was eager to take them safely out of the fort but Queen was reluctant to leave the fort and her duties. Jhalkari explained her that "there are so many soldiers fighting for Jhansi. It is the time to keep the Queen and her palace safe. There will be many soldiers but the survival of Queen is essential. If Queen becomes imprisoned by Britishers then Jhansi will be in their control."

The question was how to move the Queen out of fort. The fort was surrounded by British Army. Jhalkari suggested the Queen "give all the ornaments, crown and your clothes to me". The Queen hesitated for a while but jhalkari assured her. The plan was to take the Queen to some safe place in simple clothes. Under great protection and precaution the Queen was moved out of the fort. Then she dressed herself as the Queen and reached in front of enemy to challenge them. Jhalkari was sure the the Queen could reach a safe place with in 8 to 10 hours.

Jhalkari attacked her enemy like a braveheart. It was a great fight, the earth became red. All arms and ammunitions of the Britishers were proving futile in front of Jhalkari's war strategies. The soldiers of General Huroz ran backwards. The Commander of Durga dal proved to be a disaster. For Britishers, she was Rani Lakshmi Bai. English Army was eager to capture the Queen as they mistook Jhalkari as the Queen. Huroz was nervous. He called his mates, the antinationals of Jhansi, Peer Ali and Dulha Ju to discuss the problem with them. With the help of those traitors he wanted to find out some way to catch the Queen.

For many years Dulha ju was one of the closest to the Queen. He recognised Queen's voice, gestures and other details of her appearance. He could not be cheated. After keenly observing, he told Huroz that the person whome they thought to be the Queen is not Lakshmi Bai but, the commander of Durga Dal, Jhalkari Bai". Britishers gained there lost strength and arrested Jhalkari. They started searching for Rani Lakshmi Bai. Jhalkari was in grief. She was not prepared mentally to handover her queen to Britishers. She abused both Dulha Ju and Peer Ali with strong words. "Cowards", she said- "contemplible persons like you are the cause of our slavery. You don't have shame for cheating our Queen from whom you got love and wealth. Our queen cannot think of this type of deception from you people. To live with such stigma is worse than death in war. You won't be able to get honour from anyone. History will remember you as black spots, fraud who cheated there fair, peace loving queen Rani Lakshmi Bai. Had you been silent, history might have forgiven you. You have done a crime by exposing my plan to keep our queen safe. You won't get penance in your life. Shame on you. You deceived the person who had given you everything in life! What a brave act! You worthless creatures!"

Jhalkari gave strong lessons to the cheaters. But there was no way. She told the Britishers "If you are real men then release my handcuffs. You don't have shame to tie a lady! You call yourselves brave, in truth you are coward, and you don't have power to fight with women of India. You think yourself brave and trained soldiers? You don't have any prestige. You only know to divide and conquer. History will not forgive you".

Jhalkari was in the mercy of Britishers, but she did not want to give up easily. She asked her friend Veer Bala to kill her before the Britishers come and catch her. Veer Bala was in dilemma but at last she killed Jhalkari Bai with her sword. She is always rememberd as a lady with iron heart. A true Martyr. (1857)

★★★

For deaf people, you have to be loud

There were two bills under consideration with Government of India. One was 'Public Safety Bill' by which anyone can be arrested and jailed. The other one was 'Trade Dispute Bill' by which labourers cannot go on strike. The Central Committee of party had decided to oppose the bills. It was decided that the day government would put these bills to the Viceroy to make them law by his special authority, the two members of the party would blast a bomb, distribute pamphlets and handover themselves to police in the Assembly. Party was to select two persons amongst Jaidev Kapoor, Bhagat Singh and Batukeshwar Dutt. Finally, Bhagat Singh and Batukeshwar Dutt were selected for this task.

Jaidev Kapoor played a very important role in this mission. He used to collect permission letter every day and take his friends to watch the proceedings of the Assembly from spectators gallery. They selected the place from where they would throw the bomb. One day, Jaidev Kapoor took Chandrashekhar Azad and visited spectator's gallery as well to inspect the location properly.

Jaidev Kapoor had efficiently arranged for the permission letters to enter the Assembly Hall.

He declared himself as a student of Economics at Delhi College and wanted to consult the books at the Assembly's library. In this way, he could manage to go anywhere inside the Assembly. He made a good rapot with security officers. It was easy for him to get permission letters. Passes could be made with the letters of Congress members as well. Turn by turn, he took many revolutionaries into the Assembly hall to make a survey for the proper place in spectator's gallery.

It was the 8th April 1929, the proceedings of Assembly were going on. Suddenly, there was an explosion near the government benches. It was the sound of a bomb. Smoke spread everywhere, some benches broke and a big hole appeared on the floor.

The scene at Assembly Hall was miserable. Everyone was shouting "Bomb… Bomb…" John Simon was sitting near Vitthal Bhai Patel, the president of the Central Assembly. Suddenly Simon vanished from the place. Some of the English Men took shelter under chairs or ran towards toilet. Some members, like Pandit Motilal Nehru and Pandit Madan Mohan Malviya sat quietly.

When the smoke cleared, the public saw two youths in the spectator's gallery. They were in western clothes and smiling. The boys threw some pamphlets in the hall in which it was written- "For Deaf People You Have to Be Loud".

These two youths were Bhagat Singh and Batukeshwar Dutt.

If they wished they could have run away because it took at least half an hour for the smoke and people to settle down in the hall. Everyone was concerned about oneself, who could chase them? When the situation was under control two Sergeants came near them. Although they had revolver, they did not fire. Bhagat Singh and Batukeshwar Dutt threw their revolvers. Police arrested them. They shouted the slogans- *'Inquilab Zindabad'* and *'Samrajyavad Ka Naash Ho'*.

★★★

Netaji Subhash Chandra Bose, successfully escaped from house-arrest

(Freedom fighter Doctor Ishar Das Talwar was the brother of rebellion Hari Kishan Talwar and patriot Shri Bhagat Ram Talwar. These names are written in golden letters in the history of freedom struggle. Sri Bhagat Ram dispatched Netaji from Peshawar to Kabul and from Kabul to Berlin safely. It is written in the document.)

In the mid-night of 16th and 17th January 1941, Netaji came out by car from his residence. Althogh he was under strict vigilance of police, Doctor Shishir Bose, his nephew drove the car to Dhanbad. He had one nephew in Dhanbad who was a mining engineer. He spent one day at his home. In the evening, from Gomo station he took a train for Delhi. On the evening of 19th January 1941, he reached Peshawar by Frontier Mail. He had wore a cap on his head, a long coat, pajama and boots. Forward Block leaders and General Secretary Miyan Akbar Shah were there at the station. For the night, he had been settled in a hotel. Next day, he was shifted to a house. Afghani dress was stitched for him. On 22nd January 1941, at 6:30 in the morning, my brother Bhagat Ram Talwar took him to Khajuri Maidan of Jumbrod Road where the military camp was situated. Netaji got down before camp area and walked towards the Kabayali area by shortcut. He went to a holy place nearby where common people used to go. He moved forward and soon left the English territory before noon and entered the Kabayali land. Netaji was feeling tired. He aasked my brother to have some rest. They took rest and ate whatever they had.

My brother told him that there was no need to hurry as they were out of the British territory. Netaji became happy and rested there for a while. They reached a village by night and spent the night in a 'Hujre'. Netaji was given the name 'Mohammed Jiyauddin' and my brother 'Rehmat Khan'. Netaji was not familiar with the local language, so he tied one piece of cloth on his ears and mouth and acted like deaf and dumb person. My brother told others that he was his uncle and they were going to Adda Sharif for pilgrimage to pray for his speech and hearing.

Next day, they hired a mule and both of them preceded forward. In the evening, they took shelter in a village. Next day again, they started their journey and my brother was walking while Netaji was on a mule. The area they were crossing was hilly; Mule stumbled many times on rocks. Netaji also fell down and got injuries but they continued their journey.

People on the way told them not to take a bus or truck to Jalalabad and Kabul because there was strict vigilance on road. They took a truck but got down three miles before Jalalabad. They started to walk; my brother was a bit ahead. He saw Netaji walking and dancing with joy. When he asked him the reason of it, Netaji said "I am happy to see such beautifull mountains and dancing with joy". My brother replied- "These are barren hills with no trees, no greenery, where is the beauty?" Netaji said, The hills are beautiful because they are in a free country". One can understand the feelings of Netaji for the joy of freedom of his own country.

From Jalalabad, they took a truck and moved towards Kabul. On the way, they had to face rains and snowfall but the passion for freedom made them strong and more determined. Three miles away from Kabul city, they got down from the truck and hired a Tonga. They reached Kabul unchecked at 11 o'clock in the morning. They settled there in a Sarai. Generally the sarai were very filthy. People with camels, goats and other animals, all stayed together and the place was filled with dirt and foul smell. Netaji belonged to an aristrocrat family, still without any complaints and problems he stayed there happily and also ate their food.

He was a true patriot and his heart always pained for his bonded motherland. While he was in the Sarai, one policeman used to bother Netaji every day for money because Netaji was new at that place. My brother used to roam around High Commission offices to find the ways to send Netaji either to Russia or Germany. One day that policeman spotted a watch on Netaji's wrist, which was given to him by his father. The policeman demanded the watch and threatened him, otherwise, to take him to police station. Netaji gave him the watch without any hesitation. When my brother returned, he came to know the facts. He was worried about the security of Netaji and decided to shift him somewhere else so that nobody could recognise him. He went to search for a safe place. One day when he was passing through Bal-Labe-Daraya bazar, he saw a crockery shop and recognised its owner. He was Uttam Chand Malhotra. In 1930-31, they were jail-mates in Peshawar Central Jail. My brother entered the shop but Uttamchand could not recognise him. He asked my brother- "What do you want?" My brother replied- "I want to talk to you but in private". Uttamchand sent his servant out for another work. My brother asked him, "Do you recognise me?" he said "No". My brother told him the story that they were jail mates in Peshawar Jail, for Satyagraha Movement. He remembered my brother and hugged him with affection. He was surprised to see my brother in Kabul, he asked the reason. My brother asked him- "Do you still have the same feeling for your motherland?" He replied "Yes, why not?" My brother told him the whole story and asked him to give shelter to Netaji in his house. That time Netaji was sick due to eating breads from hotel. Uttam Chand Malhotra gladly agreed for that. Netaji was shifted to his house. Ramo Devi, wife of Uttam Chand, was a pious lady. She took utmost care of Netaji for two months.

In the meantime, my brother contacted the High Commissions of different countries. He wanted to send Netaji to Russia but Germany had attacked Russia and Russia along with France, America and Britishers in the allied forces fighting against Germany. It was the reason why Netaji was not willing to go to Russia. My brother met the High Commission officers from Italy and Germany. With their consent, he decided to send Netaji to Germany. A passport was prepared in the name of Orlando Mazzotta belonging to Sicily for Netaji and on 18th March 1941, crossing Moscow, Netaji reached Berlin. After reaching there, he organised Azad Hind Fauj in which he took the Prisoners of War, imprisoned by Germany and Italy.

Netaji planned many strategies to free the country but there was a big problem. Between Germany and India, there were so many free countries, perhaps they won't allow Azad Hind Fauj to cross their land.

Japan told Germany to send Netaji to Japan. From Japan, it was easy to attack against Britishers in India. Germany agreed and Netaji travelled by a submarine from Kil-Ki Port. He crossed Bay of Biscay, Gibraltar and the western parts of Africa. Throughout the route, there was risk of torpedo attack, but ultimately, he reached Madagascar. At Madagascar, a submarine from Japan was waiting. Netaji reached Tokyo, Japan, on 13th June 1943. He sent the message through radio to all Indians on 19th June 1943 that he had reached Japan and would attack Britishers in India very shortly to free our motherland.

★★★

Tortures could not stop them

Now the British government started worrying for those who were on hunger strike for the last 10 days, because of its consequences. It could be a problem for the government if something wrong would happen to them. It may spoil the image of their government. They started planning to do something so that the people on hunger strike neither should die nor would live a normal life. If some milk could be put forcefully in their stomach, then they won't die and would lie there like a living corpse.

They planned accordingly. A group of doctors came; the leader of the doctors was from a mental hospital whose temper was always high by treating the mental patients. He could do anything forcefully because he was used to it while treating mental patients.

The doctors were ready to apply force on starving prisoners. Approximately 10-12 strong men were included in the group to restrain the prisoners. They were also from the same jail but they all had criminal background. Most of them were Pathans with tall and huge body.

Doctors and the group of men reached the cell where Sukhdev was imprisoned. Unlocking the door, the men forwarded towards him. Sukhdev was ready for the attack. He inserted his head between two legs of a man and lifted him. The man rolled down on the floor. Like playing Kabaddi, Sukhdev was giving blow to them. Even the doctor was afraid and hid himself behind other men. At last all men jointly caught him but he slept on the floor with back above. The men forcefully made him straight. His hands, legs were pressed by four men and one of them sat on his chest. His head was pressed between the thighs of a man. The leader of the doctors went ahead and put a pipe inside his mouth. Through mouth, the pipe inserted to food pipe. By using a funnel, doctor poured milk in his stomatch. About 1 litre of milk was poured inside him.

The group of doctors and men struggled with Jaidev Kapoor to capture him. He was a strong-built man. After many attempts, they could not control him. He closed his mouth tightly. Doctor tried but ultimately he had to push the pipe through his nostril and poured milk which reached to his intestine.

The group also had opposition from Shiv Verma and Ajay Ghosh but after some struggle, they caught them and applied the same method because they also closed their mouth tightly. Their nostrils were injured due to forceful insertion.

Doctors and the group of men went to the cell of Yatindranath Das. He was already in hunger strike for 23 days from Calcutta and was aware of forceful feeding. After some struggle, the men controlled him but he closed his mouth tight. The doctor sat on his chest and inserted the pipe through his nostril. As soon as the pipe reached his throat, he coughed and due to the air pressure the pipe entered his mouth. He pressed the open tip of pipe by teeth. The doctor started pouring milk through funnel but the milk came out because the open end and was sealed by his teeth. The doctor was surprised, his clothes were wet with milk. The doctor pulled the pipe out and said,

"I will see you tomorrow, how come you don't drink milk".

Yatindranath smiled.

It was 54th day of hunger strike, Yatindranath's health was deteriorating speedly. He was vomiting, and sometimes he was getting fainted too. When he came in his senses, he lookes towards his friends. There was no complaint or sadness on his face. Only a joy of satisfaction reflected there. He said emotionally to his friends "before hunger strike I told you, victory or death. My death will be my victory. I am proud that the Great British government couldn't defeat me".

On 13th September 1929, Yatinder Nath Das had hiccups frequently and after that everything was finished silently. (1929)

★★★

He was like God to the people

Birsa Munda, the famous martyre of freedom war was born in Ulihatu (Chhota Nagpur) on 15th November 1875, 45 km from Ranchi. His father was a poor farmer. Since the family was big, so there was always financial crunch. There was no school in the village. Birsa stayed at his maternal uncle's place in Aayumatu and took care of the cattles. After staying in that village for two years, he started studying in a small school located at Aamugunu. He went to the German Mission School to attend lower primary examination. For studying in German Mission School, adoption of Christianity was compulsory. His father, with the family reluctantly converted to Christianity at

Chaibasa. After accepting Christianity, they became Masih Das and Birsa David. Unable to pronounce the name properly, his friends called him Dawood. Due to the atmosphere of the school Birsa started hating the Englishmen.

He left the membership of German Mission and went to Bangaon near Chaibasa. There he met a Vaishnav devotee; who was also a Munshi to a landlord. His name was Anand Pandey. Birsa studied Ramayan, Mahabharat, Gita and other religious books of Hinduism under the guidance of Anand Pandey. He became curious to Indian philosophy and cultural intricacies of Hinduism. Birsa secluded himself and meditated for the search of truth. He became a saint. After penance, he started spreading Hinduism and Indian culture among people. He started explaining to converted tribals that the foreign religion is not their own. He said that by adopting Christianity, we become alienated from our religion and heritage.

Birsa inspired them to fight for their rights. He objected to cow slaughter and told people to worship Tulsi. Many tribals became his followers. Gradually, he became famous as a social reformer and Saint. People started giving him the status of God.

Meanwhile, Britishers started to encroach upon the tribal community's rights with respect to the forest. Big landlords captured the forest lands. Local official and contractors started behaving badly with local tribes, as if they were slaves. Anyone with power started exploiting the tribal people. Government gave a free hand to these exploiters. City based landlords also started to seize the forest. Tribal lands were encroached. New officers began to collect the tax and court, police station were built inside the tribal locality.

When the exploitation became rampant, Birsa organised the farmers of Sirghada and Chaibasa. He filed a petition to the government. But government did not bother. The Government officials and Christian missionaries became worried by the activities of the organisation started by Birsa. To restrict them, people were arrested. Due to these arrests, there was a huge discontinent and grudge among people. To suppress the displeasure, government imposed sedition charges on many tribal people and Birsa Munda was imprisoned for two years in Hazaribagh jail. While in jail, Birsa determined to uproot the foreign government. After coming out of the jail, he organised people for armed revolution. The term used to name the revolution was "Ullu Gulan".

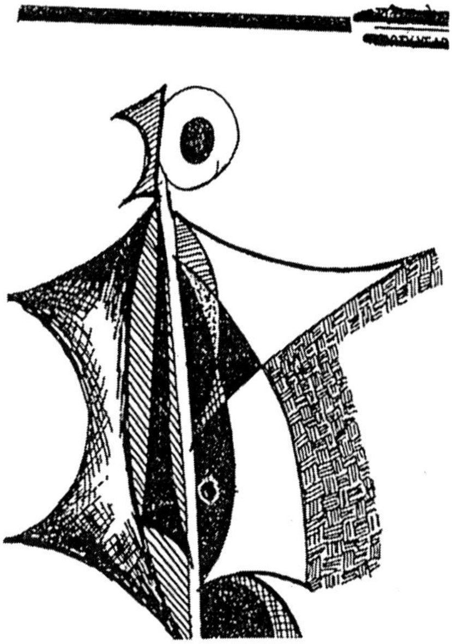

In 1899, the organised brave tribals attacked the police stations from Ranchi to Chaibasa at the same time and assaulted Englishmen with arrow and axes. To combat them, Army was deployed between Hazaribagh and Calcutta. Tribals faught bravely, but against the modern weapons their arrows and axes could not prevail. Almost 400 died and virtually the same number of tribals got arrested. Government's effort to get hold of Birsa were failure till the end. Even today, the Munda community and other tribals of Jharkhand, Orissa, Madhya Pradesh and Bihar remember the brave patriot Birsa Munda as God. (1875)

★★★

Looting of Government Treasury

The gathering of working committee of Hindustan Prajatantra Sangh was called on 7th August 1925 at Shahjahanpur on request of Ram Prasad Bismil. Rajendranath Lahiri, Sachindranath Bakshi, Manmatnath Gupta, Mukundilal Gupta, Banvarilal, Chandrashekhar Azad, Murari Lal, Keshav Chakravarti, and Ashfaqullah Khan were present in the meeting with Ram Prasad Bismil. Ram Prasad Bismil told them about the story of his train journey, in which he saw the dispatch of Government treasury. He proposed that- "we have experienced that through the simple loot we don't get much, we became the decoits and have to kill our own people. My proposal is to loot the Government treasury and I think the task is not very difficult."

Azad agreed the proposal and said- "Pandit Ji, I agree with you". We are preparing to attack Government, so this is the time to fight directly with them. They should also know that the revolutionaries are still in India, they are not sitting idealy."

9th August 1925 was decided for the train robbery and preparations were made within two days. They enquired about train time table to check when and at which station the train will halt. They decided to loot the treasury from Saharanpur-Lucknow train at Lucknow Station so that maximum amount of money can be looted. Saharanpur-Lucknow Passenger train halted at Shahjahanpur station, 7 revolutionaries boarded the train but in different compartments of the 3rd class. Bismil advised them to sit near window so they could see outside and should not talk with co passengers. This would save them from getting identified or recognized.

Someone pulled the chain. The train stopped immediately and three passengers from second class compartment got down. Rest of them also jumped down. The guard of the train got down and walked towards second class compartment from where the chain was pulled. One of the rebels held a pistol to his chest and told him to lie down or he would get killed. The British guard did the same. Other rebels from both the sides guarded the train hiding in tall grasses. They shouted to alert the passengers- "close the windows and sit quietly on your seat; don't come out of train or we will start firing."

All the passengers shut their windows closed. Driver was ordered to get down and lie on the grass. The English driver did accordingly. Bismil and Ashfaq pushed the treasure box towards the door and threw it on the ground. They tried to open it with hammer and iron rod. Sensing delay, Ashfaq took an axe and banged open the treasure box. They took all the bundles from the box and put them in a sack. By that time, the others were firing continuously. Passengers thought that a gang of dacoits were firing.

After 20-25 minutes, finishing their mission, the rebels ran away from the spot. Guard layed down on the grass. Some of the passengers got down and went to the guard. They searched for driver but the driver was not there. Ultimately he was found in the bushes. One English engineer was inside the toilet and could be brought out after much pursuation. 12 soldiers were under the seats. In total, 14 people carried guns on the train but with their accurate plan only 10 revolutionaries stole the Government treasury.

After running away from the spot, they opened the sack at one place and took out the notes from the bundles. They got 8600 rupees. They reached Lucknow with the amount and exchanged the notes. Perhaps government could declare the number of the notes. They could not change some notes because they were soiled. A few such notes were found at Shahjahanpur. Though government had already declared the numbers, so it was clear that peple from Shahjahanpur are involved in this dacoity. Ram Prasad Bismil was already under suspicion list, so government increased the vigilance on Bismil.

Government and non-government organizations were alerted by the Kakori-Train-Dacoity. It was a challenge for the Government. The police force was alert and in every state, the intellegence unit of the police were deployed.

By the looted amount, the work of revolutionaries continued effeciently. Some centres paid off their debts. Centers and party workers who needed money were given financial assistance. Some amount was kept for propaganda and rest for purchasing arms. One member of the group, who was involved in the dacoity, went to Germany and contract was given to arms dealer. Arms reached India and the amount was paid.

After this episode, the police department became very vigillant. At last, all revolutionaries were arrested. Some of them were given death sentence and some got punishment of *Kalapani*. (1925)

★★★

First warned openly, then murdered

"Freedom of India and to drive away the Britishers from India" was the main objective of the Sangh. A meeting was held at Tuticorin where Vanchi Iyer took the responsibility of killing the collector Mr. Robert William Ash. Vanchi was deputed as a clerk in the Travancore Forest Department and his friends, out of enthusiasm sent a threat-letter to Mr. Ash.

"We the members of Bharat Mata Sangh, challenge you to stop the oppressive policies towards revolutionaries; otherwise, we will chop off your head from your body and get it into picccs.

Yours
Members- Bharat Mata Sangh."

After receiving such letter, Mr. Ash and other Britishers became restless. They prepared for their own security. On 12th December 1910, the letter was handed over to the Deputy Inspector General of Police for further enquiry.

Before the murder of Mr. Ash, a zealous atmosphere was created in Southern India. A proforma titled "Vande Mataram" was distributed among the public by which youth were encouraged to kill the English people and take pledge to drive away the British empire from India.

On 17th June 1911, in such a passionate atmosphere, Vanchi got a chance to kill Mr. Ash. At around 11 o'clock in the morning Mr. Ash and his wife got down at Maniyachi station from the train coming from Tirunelveli. They were about to catch a train named 'Boat-Mail' to go to Tuticorin. One orderly was also with them. Getting down from the train, he went in the vacant first class compartment of another train standing on the platform.

The ordedly was busy with luggage. Mr. Ash started reading a newspaper. Just then, Vanchi came there and shot two bullets on Mr. Ash. He fell down and later died in the hospital.

When Vanchi shot the first bullet, people did not notice. They thought someone has opened soda bottle but when the second bullet was fired and Mrs. Ash shouted for help, then there was chaos among people. Police and public ran after Vanchi. He ran and entered the waiting hall and shot himself on his throat. He died on the spot. A letter of statement was in his pocket in which he had confessed in Tamil- "This is a pious land, where Lord Rama, Lord Krishna, Shivaji and Guru Gobind Singh ji were born and ruled. They protected each religion. But now, on such land, the Britishers are trying to make an outsider George 5th as king. So Indians are trying their level best to drive out Britishers and bringing freedom to our country."

★★★

Breaking the Salt Law

Under the leadership of Gandhiji, the Congress working committee had passed the proposal of Civil Disobedience Movement in 1930.

Gandhiji decided to break the Salt Law. With his 79 followers, he started his Dandi March from Sabarmati on 12th March. It was decided that first he would lift salt from salt area to break the law and after his arrest all Indians would do the same. As he started his journey, people got excited and joined Gandhiji. On 5th April, they reached Dandi. The same day, Gandhiji and his followers picked up salt from the sea beach and broke the Salt Law.

The whole country was awakened by this act and agitations, meetings were held everywhere. There were firing in some places. Many people died and got injured. Press Act became strict, security money was asked from the newspapers. Printing press were seized. Gandhiji gave the information to the Viceroy about controling the salt factory at Dharasana in Surat district.

On 5th May, Gandhiji was arrested. He was put in Pune jail under strict vigilance. The whole country agitated against his arrest. Total lock-down was imposed in Mumbai, Calcutta and other places. People declared their wish to discard Government status and Honours. The directive of peace and discipline given by Gandhiji was maintained. But in some places clashes between people and police took place.

The height of brutality was witnessed in North Western part where after the arrest of Abdul Gaffar Khan, Britishers brutely suppressed the non violent Pathans. At the end, the Garhwal battalion refused to shoot innocent people. As a result, punishment was given to the soldiers of the battalion with 10 to 15 years of imprisonment. The salt store of Dharasana was assaulted. Kar-bandi agitations were held at Borsad. Congress was declared illegal in June. By that time, the number of the arrested freedom fighters reached to approx. 1 lakh. A hefty fine was also imposed. Police had free hand to use Lathi and gun. They used the opportunity everywhere. Many newspapers were closed due to the heavy security deposit imposed. But one thing was clear to Britishers- people suffered a lot but never used violence as weapon. (1930)

★★★

The dangerous Revolutionary

There was a rumour in the City- "some hard core revolutionary has been caught. Attack on police is invitable." The high number of Police Force made the public panic and all shops were shut down before time.

Prithvi Singh was suffering with high fever and was fighting for his life.

He was caught on 8th October 1915. Due to fear, the police force could not keep him in hospital. On 12th October, at dead night, he was shifted to Ambala Central Jail.

The prisoners were talking about the rumours that revolutionaries have attacked the city. They can enter the jail anytime. Prithvi Singh was all alone in his cell in miserable condition but no one was there to take care of him. Prisoners were hopeful that revolutionaries would come, break the jail gate and free them. Prisoners did not know that the person who was the cause of that rumour was in the same jail in such a critical condition.

In the morning, a sweeper came into the cell. He was tall and black, with robust body. Prithvi Singh rememberd the childhood stories of jail and felt them true. He was not given any food or even water. Jail officials wanted to see the man because of whom the whole city was disturbed.

Albeit, there was Bishan Singh, the wrestler whose appearance was fearful and he was charged for decoity and murder, jail authority was not worried for him. They were worried for Prithvi Singh. They thought, he was more dangerous. Prithvi Singh was a quiet man in jail. He did his work and he was disciplined. Different cells were marked for his night stay. The guards inspected the iron rods of the prison daily. One white pot was placed in front of the cell to recognise the cell of Prithvi Singh. Every night, they used to change his cell. Even that was not sufficient, one guard used to come to the cell after every two hours and woke him up and then shout “All is Well”, that was resonated like “All is Hell”. (1915)

★★★

Spark of the Revolt of 1857

There was a plan to kick out the Britishers from India. Nana Saheb and Ajamulla Khan in North, while Rangoji Bapu in South were working hard to make the plan successful. They decided to assemble under the flag of Mughal Samrat Bahadur Shah Zafar, collectively throw out the British rigme and then give overall power of governance to Bahadur Shah Zafar. They determined that all Indians would attack the Britishers on a fixed date. They started organising a secret mission. They were sure of their success.

Before 1856, Nana Sahib started sending messages to all Kings, Nawabs and influential people of India. They sent secret proclaimers for publicity to the Indian soldiers in British Army, even to the Indian officers. The letter carried the message of freedom from the British rule and the discriminating policies towards Indians imposed by the Britishers. Nana Saheb invited them to join the fight against British rule.

Mughal Emperor Bahadur Shah Zafar and his wife supported Nana Sahib. The expelled Nawab Wajid Ali Shah of Awadh, Queen Hazrat Mahal and Minister- Ali Nabi Khan fully supported the idea of revolution. Ali Nabi Khan sent secret agents in disguise of fakirs and saints to the Indian soldiers and Army officers from Kolkata. Queen Hazrat Mahal started influencing rich and local people of Awadh to support the revolution. Thousands of Hindus and Muslim soldiers and officers took oath to participate in the battle for freedom.

There was no financial problem organising the big operation because thousands of rich people and money lenders opened their treasury to support it. Thousands of Fakirs and Sadhu's were engaged in publicity and thousands of Maulvis and Pandits started praying for the success of the revolution.

Delhi, Lucknow, Bithur, Calcutta and Satara were the main centres of conducting the operation. It was amazing! The whole India, especially the North India had become vigilant within a short span, and the Britishers knew nothing about this. Everyone kept it secret.

On March 1857, Nana Saheb and Ajamulla Khan went to Delhi from Bithur disguised as pilgrims to decide the date of starting the revolution. From Delhi, they reached Ambala and then to Lucknow. With the advices of all dignitaries, 31st May 1857 was fixed for starting the operation throughout India.

The leaders of revolution fixed two symbols for their organisation- Lotus flower and Chapati. Lotus was distributed within the platoons that were part of this organization. Chapatis were given to the watchman (*Chaukidar*) of a village. Chaukidar had a duty to eat one piece of the chapati and the rest was distributed among villages while making a fresh chapatti to be carried by the Chaukidar to the next village. It was wonder! Chapati reached through out India within a few months. Lotus and Chapati actually became very meaningful symbols.

It was unfortunate that the revolution started before the fixed date. 19th Platoon of Barrackpore refused to use the bullets containing cow and pigs fat.

The Indian officers advised them to have patience up to 31st May but Mangal Pandey was determined. When the Platoon was called for Parade on the ground, Mangal Pande jumped with his rifle and invited other soldiers. Platoon denied the order of English officer. At the end, Mangal Pandey was arrested and hanged.

On 10th May, the revolution started from Meerut, earlier than the fixed date. This was a blessing to the Britishers and curse for Indians. It is said that if the revolution had started on the fixed date all over India, there would have been no Britisher to witness the days after the revolt. And the British rule could have ended at that time only. (1857)

★★★

Let a Muslim also get an opportunity to be hanged

The case of *Kakori Kand* continued for 2 years. Bismil, Ashfaqullah, Roshan Singh and Rajendra Nath Lahiri got death sentence. As punishment, Bakshi was given lifelong imprisonment while other 18 revolutionaries got 3 years of imprisonment. With a smile on his face, Ram Prasad Bismil was hanged in Gorakhpur. The role of Ashfaqullah's sacrifice for the integrity, unity and independence of the country is unforgetable. He was born as a Pathan at Shahjahanpur. Patriotism was his passion. He always respected *Rashtra Dharm* as the biggest goal of his life and the country came foremost for him. At the time of Non Cooperation Movement by Gandhiji, he left his studies and jumped in the revolution. He was arrested for Kakori Kand and a separate case was filed against him and Sachindranath Bakshi.

Police superintendent Khan Bahadur told Ashfaq- "Listen Ashfaq, you are a Muslim and I am also a Muslim. I am depressed by your arrest. Ram Prasad is Hindu, they want to established Hindu rule. You are a learned man and belong to a high family. Don't believe these *Kafirs*. I will help you."

Ashfaq got very angry and said- "Don't you dare to speak like that. Pandit ji (Ram Prasad Bismil) and others are true Indians. They don't bother about Kingdom Governance or any Indian Government. I have heard you, I will prefer Hindu rule over Britisher. You call them *Kafir*; please get out of my sight."

One of his friends told him that he could arrange to free him from jail. Ashfaq told him- "Brother, give a chance to a Muslim also to get hanged for his motherland."

Ashfaqullah, with a smiling face read the Quran on the day of his hanging (9th December 1927). He read the Kalma throughout the way to hanging site. He kissed the hanging board and said- "My innocent hands never killed anyone. The allegations on me are totally wrong. Now I am going to Khuda to seek his justice."

He tied the rope and was hanged till death. He was a good poet. He was never scared of death. He often said-

"Bujdilon ko hee sadaa maut se darte dekha,

Garche sau baar unhein roz hee marte dekha.
Maut se veer do hamne nahin darte dekha,
Takht-ae-maut pai bhee khel hee karte dekha."
(I have seen the fearful people to fear the death,
but they die hundred times every day.
I have never seen a brave man to fear death,
on the board of death I have seen them playing.)

From Faizabad, his dead body was brought to Shahjahanpur. To seek a glimpse of his face, so many people assembled at Lucknow station. The public were weeping and crying as if there own son had left the world. (1927)

★★★

Shoot us, don't hang

Everyone was talking about Bhagat Singh and his two friends- "They are going to get death sentence but, anyhow, we should do our level best to postpone it for sometime, so we can get time to save them". This was the proposal given by Lahore Conspiracy Case-Defence Committee Lawyers. If Bhagat Singh and his friends prayed for mercy they could be saved but they knew Bhagat Singh won't do this.

Bhagat Singh had respect for advocate Prannath Mehta. On 19th March 1931, Mr. Mehta met Bhagat Singh and his friends at jail. He told them softly about Mercy Petition and assured them that- "If they say yes then he will write the petition in such a way that their honour will not become any lesser." His two friends became angry but Bhagat Singh agreed and said - "Ok, you prepare the Mercy Petition".

Mr. Mehta was very happy and after having consultation with other advocates he drafted the petition overnight. Next day, 20th March, 1931, when he reached the prison, Bhagat Singh told him that they had already sent the Mercy Petition to the Governor of Punjab and he gave the copy of petition to Mr. Prannath.

"Shoot us, don't Hang

Respected sir,

Humbly appeal to your service and wish to inform you that the British Government's highest official in India, Viceroy, by bringing a new ordinance, established a Special Tribunal to investigate the Lahore Conspiracy Case. They, on October 1930, awarded us the punishment of death by hanging. The main accusation against us is that we are at war against King George-V.

By the decision of the court two things are clear –first, there is a war between English people and Indians; second- we have certainly participated in the war. Hence, we are the prisoners of war. Although while describing so, upto some extent, it is an exaggerated statement, yet we want to mention that by doing so, we all feel honoured.

We want to shed some light on the first description. In our opinion there is no such ongoing war going on and we don't know what the court means by "ongoing war." But, we accept this decription. Along with that we want to understand it in its true meaning.

We want to state that a war is going on and it will continue till the powerful people continue to have exclusive ownership over the income and resources of people and workers. Weather such people are English ruler, English capitalists or selfish Indians. Together, they all are plundering. If the capitalist Indian sucks the blood of poor people, then it does not make any difference. Even if Government gets success by influencing some Indian leaders and heads of society; gives them some facilities and have an agreement; situation will not change. People don't get influenced much by such acts.

We don't even bother that we are ignoring and cheating the youth again. We are not scared that our political leaders are misguided and in the dialogue of compromise they have forgotten the innocent, homeless and destitute martyrs who are sadly believed to be the member of revolutionary party. Our political leaders consider them as their enemy because they believe in violence. Our warrior women sacrificed their husbands, sons and themselves but still your Government believes them to be terrorists. Your agents can malign them by making false narratives or damage the reputation of the party; but the war will continue.

It is possible that under different situations the war may take different directions. Sometimes the war will become apparent or sometime secretive; sometime widely but any how the fight will continue. Sometimes the farmers may revolt or this fight might become so dangerous that it becomes a bet for life or death. Whatever the situation is the effects of war will be on you.

It is up to you; whichever situation you choose. But, the fight will continue. Minute details will not matter. It is quite possible that the war takes a dangerous form. This will not stop till the current structure of the society is put to an end; every system is changed or revolutionized and a new age is set to start.

In near future, this war will be fought in its last phase and then it will be a decicive war. Imperialism and capitalism will only last for a while. This is the war in which we are evidently participating. We are proud to be a part of this war. We have not started the battle it will not end with our death. Our services will be recorded in the chapters of history which has been illuminated by the sacrifices of Yatindranath and Bhagwati Charan. Their sacrifices are great.

As far as our fate is concerned, we strongly want to state that you have decided to hang us, you will do exactly the same. You have the power and authority as well, but in doing so you are using the principle of being "the person with a bigger stick" and following it through. The hearing of our petition is enough to prove our point that we have never prayed to you we will not beg for your mercy. We only pray to you that according to the judgement of one of the courts of your Government we are accused of continuing the war. Your Judiciary declared us as fighter of the war.

In such case, we are the prisoners of war and on the basis of that we demand that you should treat us like prisoners of war, and accordingly, we should be shot instead of being hanged.

Now, it is up to you whether you believe in the verdict given the court of your Government. You sould give the proof of that by your actions. We humbly request you to order your Military Department to send a troop of soldiers to shoot us. (1931)

Sincerely
Bhagat Singh, Rajguru, Sukhdev"

★★★

Don’t dare to come forward

19th March 1857 was the unfortunate day for the Britishers. A brave soldier, Mangal Pandey, number 1446, of 34 Regiment of fifth company, emerged as a sun of annihilation on the ground of Barrackpore. He shouted the slogan “friends! Awake! Stand up! Don’t bother anything. Get up! Come in the name of your religion! Come ahead and give strong blow to your enemy to welcome the Goddess of Freedom.”

English Sergeant Major Hewson tried to stop Mangal Pandey. He tried to obstruct him and order Mangal Pandey to stand silently. But Mangal Pandey was not a coward; he was restless to take revenge. He unlocked his gun and shot at Hewson without any hesitation. Major Hewson fell down. He was nearing to death on the soil of India. This was the first offering of the Freedom Battle of 1857. The revolutionary year of 1857 took the first prey and the rifle of Mangal Pandey had taken the first sacrificial body with *‘Swaha’*.

Watching Hewson dying, Lieutenant Baugh came there. He was on a horse. He tried to capture Mangal Pandey. But the rifle of Mangal Pandey had become thirsty now. He shot at Baugh and he fell down from his horse. After falling down, Baugh shot Mangal Pandey from his pistol but Mangal saved himself. Baugh tried to give a blow to Mangal by his sword but Mangal cut his hand with sword from the shoulder. This was the second tribute to Goddess of Freedom.

Lieutenant Baugh was senseless. Another English man came forward towards Mangal Pandey but one of his friends assaulted the Englishman with the butt of his rifle. His head was split open.

Colonel Wheeler saw his men getting beaten. He tried to go near Mangal Pandey but Mangal roared like a lion- “Be alert! Don’t move forward! Today we will not let the body of a Brahmin be touched by your unholy hands.”

Colonel Wheeler went back. As his duty, he passed the information to the general and called for the Army.

Brave Mangal Pandey had done his duty. He thought that it was better to shoot himself rather than to be captured by the Britishers or shoot by them. He targeted on his chest and shot at, but unfortunately the bullet slipped daigonally and injured his ribs. Finally, English soldiers caught him. The Britishers tried their best to know from Mangal Pandey about others who involved in this revolution. But Mangal Pandey did not utter any name. He was Mangal Pandey; how could he bring misfortune upon his fellow revolutionaries by opening his mouth.

The Military court played the drama of justice and awarded death sentence to Mangal Pandey. To be hanged on 8th April 1857. The Hangmen of Barrackpore denied hanging Mangal. Then four Hangmen from Calcutta was later called upon to do the job. (1857).

★★★

Arms sent through toys' parcel

When Madam Cama was in Britain, she did a lot of hard work for Dadabhai Naoroji to become a member of the British Parliament. Dadabhai Naoroji was the first Indian to get elected for the British Parliament.

Madam Cama when to America and delivered speeches about the conditions in India. In November 1908, she returned back to London and sent the copies of her speeches to India. She had the slogan- "We are Indians and India is for Indians". She believed in unity and always said that no one should take the job of British Government, no matter how high the job profile is. She wished for love among humans. Once, in one of her speech, she said “It will be the happiest day of my life when I could say that the whole world is my country and every person is my relative. But before that, all countries should be made free.”

Madam Cama used to send literature to inspire the soldiers who were engaged in freedom fight. On the occasion of Christmas, she used to send arms in toy parcels. But Britishers banned her parcel and other posts. Then she started sending the posts and parcel through the French locality of Pondicherry. When an informer named Amin took the names of Sri Shyamji Krishna Verma and Sri Sardar Singh Rana related to The Browning Pistol case, they were caught by the police. The police started torturing them. Madam Cama went to the British Council in France and declared that she had sent those pistols to India. Hence, she is responsible for the act. Such a brave lady she was.

British government declared her fugitive and seized all her wealth in India, which was worth of 1 lakh. When the First World War started, then on the request of British Government, condition was imposed on her by French Government to visit the police station every week and she was sent to Bordeaux. There, her health deteriorated, but after recovering she started sending copies of Gujarati magazine “Gadar” to the revolutionaries. When First World War ended, she again started her previous work actively. She was becoming old and was not able to take active part in freedom struggle. When she was asked why she was not returning to India she replied- “Britishers want a written apology from me and also written declaration not to take any part in freedom struggle.” When she was asked “what was the problem in it? As you now too old for politics.” She objected to the view and said passionately, “I won’t be old for politics ever and still want to deliver speeches at different places in India.”

She belonged to an affluent family of diamond merchants. In the city of fashion, Paris, she never ever wore fancy dresses or beautiful sarees. She always used to wear a long gown. Her health deteriorated when she was in detention in Bordeaux for 5 years and the last days of her life were passed in poverty and illnesses. She returned to Mumbai on 1936 and died in the same year. Madam Cama inspired not just Parsi women but the women of the entire country to participate in the Freedom Fight.

★★★

Song of the masses *"Vande Mataram"*

'Vande Mataram' is not only two words; rather it is a proclamation which energizes the millions of people for achieving freedom. For centuries, it has given the message of patriotism & freedom of motherland.

On 7th August 1905, people came singing *Vande Mataram* song with slogans of Vande Mataram at Calcutta Town Hall to object Bang-Bhang Policy by which British were trying to divide Bengal into two parts. From that time, *Vande Mataram* was declaired as a slogan of rebellion and revolutionaries by the Britishers. Our Boycott and Swadeshi Movement got a proclamation and spread rapidly throughout India. We discarded the foreign items and people adopted things which were made in India. British Government was shaken by Bang-Bhang Movement. To keep the students detached from the agitation for freedom, the education department published a circular that 'if any student takes part in the Freedom Movement or utter Vande Mataram, he or she will be restricated from the school'. But the students were brave. In April 1906, in newly formed East Bengal at Barisal, a big meeting was held for thousands of people. British Government already imposed ban on *Vande Mataram* but the participants shouted *Vande Mataram* several times. Police had beaten them furiously but the sloganeering did not stop.

By this time, the slogan of *Vande Mataram* had spread throughout the country. In 1905 at Indian National Congress meeting, *Vande Mataram* was accepted as a song to be sung in every National meeting. On this ocassion, it was advised to alter the song a bit. In place of seven crores (population of Bengal at that time), 30 crores (population of India at that time) were recommended to be used.

On November 1906 in Dhuliya, *Vande Mataram* was sung with the procession. When Lokmanya Gangadhar Tilak was arrested in 1908 and sent to Mandalay (now in Myanmar), the public chanted *Vande Mataram* even though it was banned. Some of them were beaten badly for this and others were arrested.

In 1907 when the youth shouted *Vande Mataram* at Lahore in protest of the arrest of leaders, they also faced the brutality of police. In February 1908 at Tuticorin, Tamil Nadu, the labourers of Coral Mills shouted *Vande Mataram* against

British ownership of companies, to show the solidarity from opression, they were assaulted by the police. In Tirunelveli, the police gave the same treatment to the people taking out protest marches with loud chants of *Vande Mataram*. Even the British people residing, there were forced to chant *Vande Mataram.*

After sometime, *Vande Mataram* crossed the border of India and was used outside also. In 1901, when Madan Lal Dhingra was prosecuted for shooting an English man in England, he also shouted *Vande Mataram* at the time of hanging. A magazine was published by the name of '*Vande Mataram*' in 1909 in Paris. In its first edition, they wrote about the movement against the atrocities of Britishers in Bengal. In this way, *Vande Mataram* became the sign and symbol of the revolution.

★★★

Get revenge of killing

"Saunders had beaten Lala Lajpat Rai so badly that he died due to his injuries. We are going to take revenge of his death from Saunders. Now you keep quiet, I will plan it within one or two days then give you the responsibility".

After two days, Azad worked on the plan and finalised it. On 17th December 1928, they reached the police station where J.P. Saunders, the Assistant Superintendent of Police used to work, near DAV College.

There was a road between DAV College and the police station. Jai Gopal started pretending to repair his cycle on the road. His task was to identify Saunders. When Saunders would come out, he would stand up. Bhagat Singh and Rajguru were standing near the Police Station and started general gossip between them as if they were students. They were waiting for the signal from Jai Gopal. Chandrashekhar Azad had hidden himself behind a pillar of the college gate, ready with a Mouser gun in his pocket. His task was to check anyone coming after Bhagat Singh and Rajguru after they had killed Saunders. On 3rd stage of the plan, Bhagwan Das Mahur and Vijay Kumar Sinha were kept ready to fight besides their friends in case the encounter became challenging.

In the evening, exactly at 5 o'clock, Saunders rode a motorcycle and came out of police station. Jai Gopal stood up at his place. Bhagat Singh and Rajguru were prepared. Bhagat Singh thought- let him come near. But Rajguru thought Bhagat Singh was hesitating to shoot the bullets. He jumped in front of Bhagat Singh and shot Saunders. The bullet penetrated the head of Saunders. He fell down immediately from the motorcycle. Bhagat Singh shot four bullets on his body to confirm his death. In between, the extra magazine of Bhagat Singh's gun dropped there. Bhagat Singh returned back, but Rajguru went ahead to pick that magazine. Azad shouted from behind the pillar-

"Come here, why are you going there to die?"

Rajguru returned only after picking Bhagat Singh's magazine. In the mean time, the sound of bullets alerted the entire police station. One English officer Mr. Fern jumped there and found the revolver of the murderer as empty. He tried to catch Bhagat Singh alive but Rajguru pushed him aside and came in the hands of Fern. After seeing Bhagat Singh safe, he lifted Fern and threw him on the road. Fern was badly injured. Even he couldn't stand up.

Then three police personnel chased Bhagat Singh and Rajguru. Azad challenged them. Two of them returned but Havildar Chanan Singh kept moving on. Azad thought if he fires the bullet, it could strike Bhagat Singh or Rajguru. But he took the shot very carefully and it hit a leg of Chanan Singh. Charan

Singh still continued to run. Now Azad shouted- "I don't want to kill any Hindustani but if you are so eager to die, then ok."

Azad fired at Chanan Singh with his Mouser pistol on his chest and he died on the spot.

Chandrashekhar Azad, Bhagat Singh and Rajguru were in the campus of the college. They waited for sometime in apprehension of any danger. They had hidden their cycle at the back of the college. When no one came, they took the cycle and reached Mozang-house. Other comrades also reached there safely. A successful mission was completed under the guidance of Azad. Next day, it was written on the walls of Lahore "Saunders, who killed Lala Lajpat Rai, has been killed and we have taken the revenge".

★★★

Spark of Revolution

Indian freedom fight was a Ganga-Jamuni confluence of armed and non violent revolutions. From the beginning of British imperialism, Indians were restless to save their identity. The fight started with the Battle of Plassey against British in 1757. It was a failed attempt but the country did not keep quite. The Sages and Fakirs left their holy beads, picked swords and jumped into the freedom movement. Between 1663-76 the leader of Fakirs, Shekh Manju, made it difficult for the Government to administer Rajshahi, Rangpur, Purnia, Dinajpur, Pabna and Dhaka. British Government could not control or catch them. Hermits' leader Bhawani Pathak and Mohan Giri fought with the soldiers of East India Company many times.

The spark of revolution kept burnig from 1757 to 1857. By 1857, the whole country prepared itself for the struggle against the Britishers. Mangal Pandey started the revolt and the fire of revolution spread to Delhi, Meerut cantt. The Revolutionary soldiers caught hold of Delhi and reinstated Bahadur Shah Zafar as the head of Delhi. But unfortunately, the betrayal by insiders did not provide permanent results. The foundation of British imperialism was shaken by the revolt of 1857. Nana Sahib Peshwa guided the revolution. He organised all Rajas and Maharajas under one umbrella. The secret agents in the disguise of Sadhus and Fakirs inspired local people for revolution. Lotus and chapati were made the symbols of unity and sacrifice. The outburst of armed revolution made Britishers worried. But as always, they got the support of traitors and the whole effort became a failed affair.

All though in 1857, the revolution failed; atrocity and discrimination amplified but the flame of freedom fight in Indians was still burning. Wahabi Movement emerged in Bengal but it was brutally suppressed. A group of Sikhs, under the leadership of Ram Singh, organized an Army in Punjab. They were called *Kuka*. Kuka people established a parallel government in 23 districts of Punjab. Their plans being exposed before proper execution, got them crushed them brutaly.

After sometim, the armed revolutions took place but organized battles were stopped. Lord Curzon announced Bang-Bhang. The whole Bengal was in termoil. Revolutionaries took arms to oppose this policy. Bombs exploded at several places. By spreading terrorism they tried to disturb the Government functionaries.

In 1914, the First World War was going on. Britishers were busy in the war. Revolutionaries took the opportunity; they combined army and public on same platform igniting the flame of total freedom and started armed revolution. Ras Bihari Bose from Bengal organised revolutionaries of Bengal, Punjab and

Uttar Pradesh. Sachindranath Sanyal helped him. Indian residents abroad gave momentum to this revolution. On 19th February, 1915, camps were completely ready for massive revolt. But like earlier, a traitor Kripal gave up all the secrets to the Britishers and they crushed it brutally, and every preparation for combined revolution was ruined.

Then came the time of Bhagat Singh and Chandrashekhar Azad. From 1925 to 1931, they were the centres of revolution. All India Revolutionary Organisation was established. Women played a remarkable role in this revolution.

1931 to 1946 was the Gandhian era, in which the agitation was based on non violence. It picked up its pace, armed revolutions were neutral. The mass movement of 1942 was a combined effort of Naram dal and Garam dal (revolutionaries and non violent followers) and in the meantime, Lokmanya Tilak took the centre stage for Garam dal. Netaji Subhash Chandra Bose organised Azad Hind Fauj. Although it could not get expected result, it affected people deeply. The foundation of imperialism became weak. In 1946, the Naval Mutiny harmed the already weakened roots of British Kingdom. The denial of army to fight

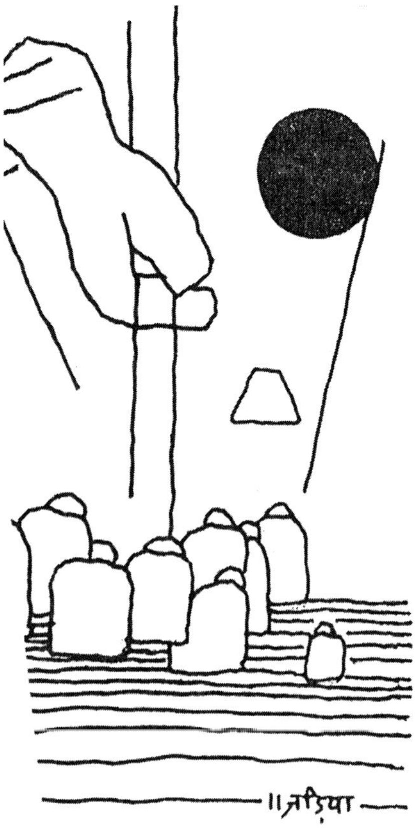

against Rebels clearly acknowledged the departure of Britishers. The then Prime Minister of England Attlee accepted that they were going to submit the Government of India to Indian people because Indian Army was no longer loyal to British authority and Britain was unable to keep big English Army to fight with the Indian Army.

Actually, the armed revolution made the British Kingdom hollow from inside and it further crumbled because of the non violent agitations.

We have the responsibility to build a progressive nation and should not forget the sacrifices of patriots who fought to bring freedom to our country. If we don't devote us to the progress of our country, it would be an injustice to the martyrs and patriots who brought freedom to us.

★★★

Their mission accomplished

The revolutionaries of Nashik had plans to kill the Collector Jackson. To make it happen, Anant Lakshman Kanhare, a young boy was most excited. Kanhare was a member of Abhinav Bharat Sanstha and lived in Aurangabad. His wish was to kill Jackson in the same way as Madan Lal Dhingra killed William Hutt Curzon in London. He wanted to give Britishers a lesson that "Indian youth never defers from there objective. Whatever the circumstances may be, they are prepared and not afraid of anything". To give its proof, he held his hand on burning flame for two minutes.

21st December 1909 was fixed for Jackson's assassination. He had been transfered to Pune. On 21st December 1909, the officials organized a farewell function at Vijayanand Hall of Nashik and also arranged the play "Sharda" to be perform.

Anant Lakshman and his friends took seats in the hall. In Vinayak Narayan Deshpande's house, they all had a meeting and arms were distributed among the youth. Anant Lakshman had a Browning pistol which was brought by Chaturbhuj Amin from London. Beside that he was given a nickel plated pistol. It was decided that if he misses the target, Deshpande will fire and then Krishna Gopal Karve will fire. The seat allotted to Jackson was near to Anant Lakshman.

At schedule time, Jackson reached the hall. He was walking at the front of other people followed him. As soon as he crossed Anant Lakshman, he fired from the pistol. But he missed it. In the next moment, he fired the second time which injured the arm of Jackson. The public presumed it was the sound of crackers but when Jackson fell down, they understood the matter. When Jackson fell down Anant Lakshman fired several times and he died on the spot. Rather to get farewell from Nashik, he got the farewell from the world.

★★★

Killed at hospital

On August 29th, 1930, at 9:15 a.m., Inspector-General of Police of Bengal was killed by the rebels. When the revolutionaries of Dhaka got the information that F.J. Lowman, Inspector-General of Police was visiting Dhaka, they became active. How was it possible that the Inspector-General of Police was coming to their city and they won't welcome him properly? Lowman was a famous person but he was not like a flower he was like a thorn, which always pricked in the hearts of these revolutionaries. They wanted to crush the thorn. They had a secret meeting and planned the future for Mr. Lowman. Binoy Bose took the responsibility of killing Lowman. He was given several bullets and two guns.

The Superintendent of Prison-Police of Narayanganj was sick and admitted to Mitford Hospital of Dhaka. Mr. Lawman was to visit him. He reached Dhaka and with the Police Commissioner of Dhaka, Mr. Hudson, reached the hospital. Mr. Lawman and Mr. Hudson were talking while walking inside the premises of hospital. Suddenly, a young man came running towards them from a distance of around 50 feet and started firing. The youth shot five bullets. Three of the bullets hit Hudson and two hit Lowman. The young man was Binoy Bose.

Binay Bose came as thunder and ran away. One person caught him but he escaped. Near the outer wall, he left his shoes and fired one bullet at the people chasing him. No one was hurt but they stopped for a while. He left empty revolver there and jumped the wall. Some people still tried to catch him but he saved himself by firing with the second revolver. Ultimately he was out of reach.

The Police were frustrated. They could not catch the murderer. They played the sly act to save their skin from the stigma. They put alligation on the students of medical college hostel stating that they helped the killer to get away. Around 50 students living in hostel were so mercilessly beaten that they were to be hospitalised.

★★★

Don't let the fire of revolution extinguish

The same Hudson, who arrested Bahadur Shah Zafar, killed his sons and also drank their blood, went to imprisoned Nahar Singh and proposed friendship on behalf of Britishers. Nahar Singh knew the brutality of Hudson. Hudson told Nahar Singh- "I am going to save you from being hanged; bend a little".

Nahar Singh turned his back to Hudson and replied- "Nahar Singh is not a traitor who will surrender before enemy. English people are enemy of my country. I cannot beg their pardon. If one Nahar Singh dies, millions of Nahar Singh will be born".

Major Hudson got furious. He planned to hang him publicly. The middle of Chandni Chowk was selected for hanging so that the passer-by could witness the death of a king. The residence of Nahar Singh was nearby. Britishers had chosen the day of the birthday of Nahar Singh for his hanging. He was going to complete 35 years on that day. The public of Delhi witnessed the event with tears in their eyes. Nahar Singh was a very popular king.

Before hanging to Nahar Singh, Hudson asked him his last wish. Raja replied- "I don't want to lose my esteem asking you people anything. I only tell my fellow country men that don't allow the flame of revolution to be extinguished." (1857)

★★★

Snatched arms from the police & dacoity

Alluri Sitarama Raju left his sainthood. He stopped giving religious speeches in temples and singing *Keertans*. He collected the tribals of Andhra Pradesh and started organising an army. He developed the organisation very fast as the local people regarded him as God. He always advocated for the betterment of people and society. People believed his political views and joined his army.

It was surprising that a boy brought up in a collector's house became a rebel. He was born on 4th July 1897 near Visakhapatnam, in a village. He studied Sanskrit and English. In the same manner, he organised an army by his own efforts and conducted the soldiers' training. The whole Rampa area was the centre of his activities.

Collecting weapons for his army was a challenge for Raju. Although they had bows and arrows, it was not sufficient to fight with the British Police Force. He knew that either he had to purchase them or to loot them from police station. He started decoity for money to purchase weapons and snatched weapons from police station.

The first big success for him was when he attacked on Chintapalli police station in Rampa area. Around 300 comrades helped him. He collected a huge number of Rifles. The second assault was on Krishnadevipeta police station. From there, he collected several arms. The attack on police station was going on continuously.

His attacks made the Police and Government alert. At first, he was considered a petty dacoit but after sometime they came to know the reality that he planned to overthrow the British Empire with his army. Then the British empire deputed the two

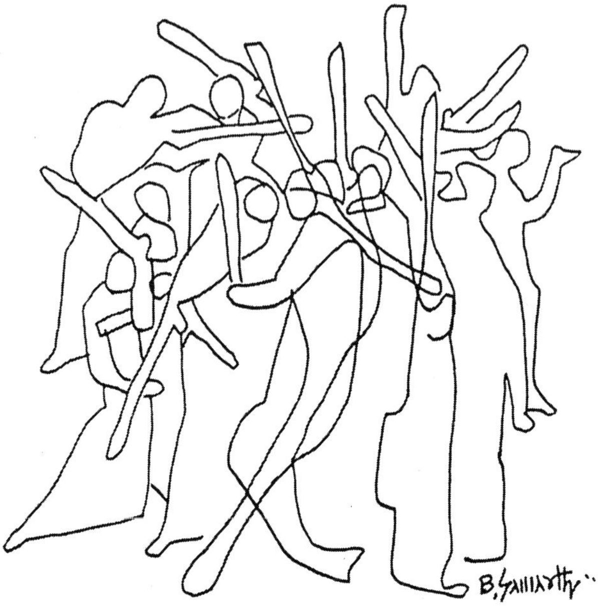

lieutenants, Scott and Ayar, to kill him. They attacked Raju and his army on 24th September 1922. There was a big hue and cry but in that battle, Scott and Ayyar were killed and many soldiers also lost their lives.

With this success of his own, Raju distributed pamphlets in public to warn Britishers to leave Andhra-bhoomi at once. But Britishers were not ready to leave so easily. Rather they started searching for Raju in a more vigourous manner. They even declared a reward of 10000 Rupees for the information or capture of Raju. Britishers spent lacs of rupees to control Raju.

At the foothill of Mampa Hills, Raju was busy cleaning blood spots from his body, at that time only the Britishers came to know about his whereabout through their spies. Under the leadership of Goodal, the Army surrounded him. Soldiers fired excessively. Patriot Raju uttered *'Vande Mataram'* and closed his eyes on 7th May 1924.

★★★

As Thought, so Did

Indian National Association was celebrating its annual day function on 1st July 1909. Madanlal met Kumari Emma Josephiel and pleased to know that Curzon Wyllie was also coming for the celebration.

On that date, Madan Lal had his dinner earlier and reached to his shooting club. He practiced firing the shots and got self-satisfaction.

From the Shooting club, Madanlal reached his room and chaned his attire. He dressed up in a beautiful suit and tie for the celebration and tied a sky blue *Saafa* on his head. He put on dark goggles on his eyes. He kept two loaded revolvers, concealed in his pockets. He hid two knives in pockets as well. He started from his house, fully equipped to kill the enemy for the mother of freedom.

Bhartiya Rashtriy Sansthan was celebrating its annual function at Imperial Institute's Jahangir hall. He reached there at 8 p.m. and met Kumari Emma. She was pleased to see Madan Lal. All the time he was busy chatting with his friends but kept a watch at the door from where Curzon Wyllie was to enter. In the meantime, cultural program was going on.

At 10 p.m., Curzon Wyllie entered the hall with his wife. People were happy to see him at the function. The program ended at 11 p.m. Curzon met some Indian youths. He said "hello" to Madan Lal. Madan Lal took the opportunity and went near him. Curzon was standing on the step of the stage and wanted to ask something to Madan Lal. Curzon bent towards Madan Lal, taking this opportunity Madan Lal fired on his chest. Curzon cried and fell down on the steps. Madan Lal fired thrice on his face. His eyes popped out and face was disfigured. Cowasji Lalkaka, an Indian Parsi man rushed towards Madan Lal to catch hold him, but Madan Lal shot him with the last bullet. Cowasji died two days later. Meanwhile, many people rushed to Madan Lal and caught him. One loaded revolver and two knives were found in his pocket. Madan Lal did not want to hear anyone. Curzon Wyllie died on the spot.

Police reached there and arrested Madan Lal Dhingra. He was quiet, as if nothing unusual happened. He lifted his goggles from the floor and wore it; one doctor was called to check upon him. The doctor was trembling with fear. After the arrest of Madan Lal, he only said that to shoot Cowasji Lalkaka was not his intention, he shot him to save himself. Madan Lal had a written message with him. On checking him, the police found it but they did not disclose it. Althoudh Madan Lal had already left a copy of his statement with Savarkar.

Next day, the news of the killing of Curzon Wyllie was published in the newspapers of London. Entire England was numb in shock. The news reached India in a while. Patriot Indians and revolutionaries felt pride after this news.

★★★

Devastation by a Revolutionary

The reporter of London Times wrote an article to evaluate Tatya Tope's plans. It was written-

"Our very friend Tatya is distressful and a shrewd enemy. I am short of words to elaborate his qualities. Since last June, he has spread turmoil in Central India. He crushed our palaces, looted our treasury, and emptied our magazines. He collected army and dug up trenches. He fought against kings and snatched their cannons. His movements are like electric current - sometimes at this side of Narmada, sometimes on the other side. He walks 30 to 40 miles per day. He walked through our soldiers from left & right, from back & front, from mountains & rivers, from valleys & hills but never controled or caught by our army."

While attacking, Tatya Tope would get aggressive like a lion and tear apart the enemy like Hyenas. If he was surrounded by enemy, he will fly away like a soul from body. It is impossible to explain his entire journey, cunning moves, his wins and his defeats in words.

Tatya: a great warrier

On 18th April 1859 at 4 p.m., he was taken to the execution ground. Repeatedly, he said to the English officers that his aged father was innocent, he should not be bothered.

Without any hesitation, bravely he climbed the stairs of execution site.

He declined covering his face. He said that it was not required and he was ready to face his death. No face cover and his hands and legs were also not tied. He himself pulled the noose around his neck. The handle was pulled and within no time the platform displaced and his body was hanging with the rope, and it was left hanging till the sunset.

English officers took away the hairs of Tatya. Even today the hairs of Tatya are exhibited in England and the story of his bravery is told and discussed.

Scared of Tatya's name

English people were eager to catchhold of Tatya. He was very swift. In a fraction of moment, he disappeared from the scene. English people would shiver by the name of Tatya. He used to fight like a wild lion. Within a short period, he fought with the Britishers for more than 150 times. His sword chopped the heads of many English Generals and thousands of soldiers of the Britishs Army knelt down before him. After the end of revolt, when he went for hiding in the forest, his friend Maan Singh cheated him, for a petty piece of land, and informed the Britisher about Tatya. They framed the cases of murder and loot on him, and then ultimately hanged on 18th April 1859.

★★★

Consumed blood mixed water

The Police aimed to capture the accomplices of the revolutionaries who escaped at the time of raid. A special person was deputed for that work. Bhupendranath Chatterjee, special police officer, from the Intelligence Department, was given this task. Bhupendranath Chatterjee was a shrewd officer. He routinely walked around the jail after his office hours.

Bhupendranath Chatterjee also tried to break the unity among rebels with divide and rule policy. The revolutionaries understood his game but were afraid of his sly nature. They decided to end the fear by killing him. Bhupendranath was aware of this and so he always kept his security tight.

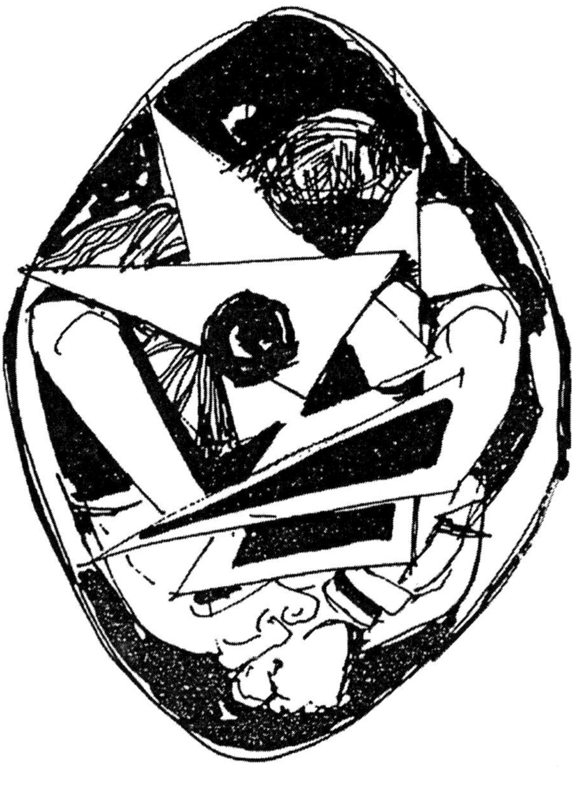

On 28th May 1926, it was evening time and Bhupendranath was on the way to inspect the jail. On a regular basis, he would speak to the prisoners of the cells, which were in his route. Ananthari, an accused of the bomb blast case, and his friends decided to teach a lesson to Bhupendranath. They asked the warden to open their cell as ours one *dhoti* had fallen in the gutter and they would bring that. Warden agreed and opened the cell lock. As soon as the lock opened, Ananthari lunged towards Bhupendranath and gave a hard stroke on his head with an iron rod. Bhupendranath's head was split and he got unconscious. They kept beating him furiously. Ultimately, Bhupendranath died.

They left Bhupendranath there and came back to their cell and threatened the warden not to speak about the incident or he would be punished in the same manner. The warden rang the warning bell loudly but by that time revolutionaries washed off all the evidences. Ananthari Mitra washed his blood stained hands in a plate and also the iron rod. Now the problem was that where to throw the blood-mixed water in the plate, for that, Ananthari drank the blood-mixed water like as Bhimsen who drank the blood of Dushasan in the Mahabharata, and thus destroyed all the evidences of murder. Also, he placed the iron rod as it was kept.

★★★

Wrote poems before hanging

There was a great agitation by the public to dismiss the order of hanging for the revolutionaries. The Members of Central Assembly wrote an application, signed by all members, and put it before senior *Laat-Sahib*. Dates of hanging were postponed twice. People thought it was a good sign and might be their hanging would be cancelled. But Britishers were after the blood of the revolutionaries and they were adamant. So, executions were made.

Pandit Ram Prasad Bismil was hanged on 19th December 1927. On the evening of 18th, when he was given a glass of milk, he denied and said he would drink his mother's milk tomorrow. Next morning, after routine chores and Pooja, he wrote a letter to his mother, in which he wrote a message for all the fellow Indians. Then he calmly sat and waited for his hanging. When the jail persons came to take him towards the execution platform, he immedietely stood up and shouted *"Vande Mataram"* and *"Bharat Mata ki Jai"* and walked with them. He recited a poem also-

'Malik teri raza rahe aur tu he tu rahe,
Baki na main rahun, na meri aarzu rahe.
Jab tak ki tan mein jaan, ragon mein lahu rahe,
Tera he zikr ya teri he justhju rahe.'

Reaching at the door of Hanging cell, he said- "I want complete destruction of British Kingdom." Reciting prayers at the last moment- ***"Vishvani Dev Savitarduritani..."*** he was hanged till death at Gorakhpur jail.

There was strict security around the prison at the time of his execution. Local public gave a mournful farewell to his body. People offered flowers and scents to the body and last rites were done with full honour. Before hanging, he sent a letter to one of his friends. He wrote-

"Whatever is going to happen on 19th December 1921, I am fully prepared for it. It is nothing but changing of the body. I believe that I will return soon to serve my motherland again with full energy and enthusiasm."

"Yadi desh hit marna pade mujhko sahasro baar bhi.
To bhi na main is kasht ko nij dhyan main laaun kabhi.
Hey ish! Bharatvarsh mein saat baar mera janm ho.
Kaaran sada he mrityu ka deshopkarak karm ho,
Marte Bismil, Roshan, Lahari, Ashfaq atyachar se.
Honge paida saikdon unke rudhir ki dhaar se.
Unke prabal udyog se uddhaar hoga desh ka.
Tab naash hoga sarvada dukh shok ke lovelesh ka.
My salutation to all."

Bismil was a very good poet. Once he wrote a poem when he was jailed, which expresses his patriotic feelings towards his motherland. It was published at Lucknow in newspaper 'Awadh' by the permission of Syed Enuddin. So, we are narrating it as follow-

"Mit gaya jab mitane wala fir salam aaya to kya?
Dil ki barbadi ke baad uska payaam aaya to kya?
Kaash apni zindagi mein hum yah manzar dekhte,
Yun sare-turbat koi maheshar kharam aaya to kya?
Mit gayi jumla ummiden, jata raha saara khyaal,
Us ghadi fir naambaar lekar payaam aaya to kya?
Ae dile naakaam mit jaa, ab to kooche-maar mein,
Fir meri naakaamiyon ke bad kaam aaya to kya?
Aakhri shav deed ke kabil thee, "Bismil" ki tadap,
Subah dam gar koi bhi baalaae baam aaya to kya?"

★★★

Blood for Blood

In the "Old Bailey Criminal Court", London, the spectators were waiting eagerly for an Indian who killed an English high official on the land of England to take revenge for his deeds in India.

When the huge man standing like in the wooden court-stand stared towards the gathering of people like a victor, spectators started whispering about the extraordinary looking man.

"He looks like a mountain of collyrium".

"I don't want to see Indian lion after watching him".

"He does not look like a murderer".

"He knows, he is going to die but still so cheerful".

By the order of the judge, everyone became silent. Judge asked the neutral looking Udham Singh "Do you have anything to say?"

When the judge was asking from him, his boldness and fearless stature was really daring.

"Why did you kill Sir Michael Francis O'Dwyer? What type of enmity did you have with him?"

Udham Singh replied, "I have seen the mass slaughter at Jallianwala Bagh, Thousands of men, women and children were forcefully killed there without any reason. I am also a human being and certainly it affected me. At that time, I took the oath to kill General Dwyer any how. But when I reached here he was already dead. Now only Lieutenant Governor Sir Michael O'Dwyer was left from whom I could take the revenge for killing. I hated both of them. Even the British Kingdom is also a matter of hatred for me."

The judge asked him- "Why could you not get the incident out of your heart for last 20 years?"

Udham Singh replied- "How could I? Yes, it was impossible for me to forget what I had seen. I never forgot the grusome cruelity and oppression. Now, after 21 years, I am happy that I bet my life but took the revenge. I am glad to have presented my insignificant life at the feet of my motherland."

England thought that India has forgoten about the incident of Jallianwala Bagh but they were mistaken. To take revenge of the heinous incident, a child took the oath because he had witnessed the crime and he was just 12 years old. That child was Udham Singh. So, to take revenge, Udham Singh came to England to study engineering.

On 12th June 1940, the British government in England declared execution for Udham Singh. He was a great martyr, still remembered with honour as legend.

★★★

She was more than a flame

"Look girl! See your age! Why are you spoiling your life? Just provide us the information of revolutionaries. We will release you and offer you a big reward."

"My sacrifice will be my reward. Being a true revolutionary, I don't fear death. My duty towards my motherland cannot be wavered with money or death threat. My death will be the reason for the end of British Kingdom."

Mr. Outram was furious after listening about the downfall of British empirefrom this little girl. He ordered his soldiers to tie the girl with a tree, make ready her pyre, and ignite it. The soldiers followed their General's order. When the flames reached the face of Maina, Outram again said- "Still there is time to save yourself. Just tell us your father's whereabouts. We can save you."

Maina gave a befitting reply, "It's only one birth, even if you burn me in several births, I won't tell you the secrets of my father and other revolutionaries. The Indian women warriors feel the fire flames as cold as the sandlewood. But remember one thing that your last days have come, and your atrocity will drawn you to hell.

Maina stood straight and the flames raised high. Was she herself less than a flame? (1857)

★★★

A petty servant has done a big job

A crazy man came to the waiter of the Resident for a job. He told him that he can cook and clean utensils, and do other works also skillfully. The waiter thought that he seemed as a clown, we could assign him some job and he would entertain us as well. So he kept him for dish-washing job, but offered him only food in exchange of his service, without any salary.

The mad man used to get dirty while washing utensils and made funny movements to entertain other servants. Sometimes he brought vegetables from the bazar. He was considcrcd good at bargaining.

By then, many articles came against the Resident in *Amrit Bazar Patrika*. The Resident came to know that somebody was sending the article from Bhopal and tried to create an atmosphere against him. He declared that if anyone could catch the informer, he would be given a huge amount. The police was restless but they could not catch the person.

The atmosphere against the Resident deteriorated day by day. The Government intervened and transferred the Resident from Bhopal. The Resident gave parting gifts to every servant including the eccentric man.

The Resident left Bhopal and made temporary arrangements to stay in Delhi for some time. One day a dark man wearing suit came to visit him. He spoke in English fluently. The Resident was astonished that he was the same eccentric man who worked as a servent in his bunglaw and washed his utensils.

The man started speaking in English.

"*Saheb*, I've come to collect my reward."

"I had already given reward to everyone while coming from Bhopal."

"*Saheb,* you told about the reward which would be given to the man who would reveal the secret spy."

"Yes, I did say so, but we could not identify or catch him.

"Can you help us to catch him?" said the Resident.

"*Saheb*, I am the same guy who lived in the quarters outside your bunglaw and provided secrets to 'Amrit Bazaar Patrika'." The man said.

Resident was trembling in fear now. He knew about the daring acts of revolutionaries. He was afraid for his life. He thought what if this man has come not to take the reward but has come to give me the reward of death. To save himself, the Resident took out his watch with the golden chain and offered it to the man. He told the man that if he wants he would be given a job at a high position in Secret Service Department with a monthly salary of 1000 rupees.

The man replied- "If I wanted money, then why would I have worked without salary at your place?"

"What do you want to do now?" Sahib asked.

"Now I want to kill other brutal officers like you."

The man replied calmly and left from there.

He was the famous revolutionary Sufi Amba Prasad. (1890)

★★★

When chopped his limbs

Deputy Commissioner Mr. Cowan of Ludhiana arranged cannons at the crossroads of Malerkotla town. *Kuka* folks (revolutionaries) were tied infront of the mouth of cannons; the cannon wik was ignited and they blasted in pieces. Out of 50, 49 kuka people died. The last of the Kukas was a child of 13 years. His mother urged to Mrs. Cowan to spare the child. Mrs. Cowan was there as a witness to the event. On her recommendation, Mr. Cowan agreed to spare the boy named Bishan Singh.

"We will spare you, but you have to leave your shrewd Guru Ram Singh." Cowan told him.

As soon as Bishan Singh heard bad words about his Guru, he became ferocious. He lifted Mr. Cowan and thrashed him on ground. He sat on his chest and pulled his beard. He repeatedly thumped his head on the ground. Soldiers tried to save their officer from the clutches of the boy but could not succeed. Ultimately, they amputated both the hands of the child from his shoulders and his legs were chopped off as well.

This is the story of a 13-year-old child who fought bravely and died for his motherland. (1875)

★★★

When blisters were oozing

Fed up with Indubhushan, the jail authorities of Andaman jail gave him permission to work. But to take revenge, they ordered him so much of work that it was impossible for one man. His task was to crush poisonous bushy plants and make ropes from them. While crushing the plants, the poison gave blisters in his palms and hands. The blisters exploded and liquid oozed out. He was unable to do anything. He could not even eat properly. It was a very painful condition. He almost quit eating.

Indubhushan asked jail authorities to give him some other work because the blisters and the pain were unbearable. The jailer was irritated from the beginning; he abused him and asked him to pull the *Kolhu* to squeeze out oil. The task was even more difficult. With exploding blisters in hand, he pulled the *Kolhu*. It was a nonstop job, and he was whipped for stopping or being careless even for a moment.

Indubhushan appealed to the authority to admit him in jail hospital for treatment. He assured the authority that he will do any work given to him after his treatment. But the appeal was not approved by the jailer. Instead, the jailer increased the quota of oil that he had to squeeze out from *Kolhu*. At the time of inspection, he was told by the jailer that if he fails to draw the stipulated amount of oil, he will be beaten by an executioner with a whip.

To get rid of this type of insult and pain, Indhubhushan had only one choice, which was to commit suicide. But it was not easy in the jail. He saw a hook on the roof of his cell but there was no rope. One night, he took off his clothes and tore them into pieces. With those pieces, he made a rope and hanged himself making a loop of the rope.

How ridiculous it was! The British Court accepted the statement of the jailer that Indubhushan was afraid of getting murdered by his fellow inmates and that's why he committed suicide. (1933).

★★★

Who says Hindustan won't be free

In the morning, the soldiers of Azad Hind Fauj paraded perfectly. The soldiers told their wives that today they were going to weigh Netaji with gold. Netaji was sitting on one side of the 'weighing balance' which was draped with tricolor flowers and on other side women came and dropped their offerings. One Bengali doctor's family from Malaya blew their conch shells and inaugurated the event. A Gujarati lady offered 5 bricks of gold on the balance. Gradually, women came from every direction and donated ornaments of gold, and silver. Evcn diamond and costly stones were offered.

Women were coming with their belongings either in bags or in handkerchief. They offered and joined hands before Netaji. It was an amazing scene. The sound of *Jai Hind* and *Inqlaab Zindabad* were mixed with the sound of conch. The weighing balance was full but it was not sufficient. Soldiers said to the gathering "we need more gold".

The ladies offered whatever they were wearing, their earrings, bangles, chains etc. on the balance. One lady offered her gold watch. But still the weight was not equal.

In the meantime, a sound of weeping came from the crowd. Everyone was astonished. Commander Lakshmibai came with a lady before Netaji. She told Netaji that her husband was martyred in the war recently. Subhash Chandra lifted his cap and said- "Sister, God is also eager to take the place of your husband. I am your brother". The lady gave her *mangalsutra* on balance but still it was not sufficient.

One old lady came to the spot. She was having a photo with golden frame. She told Netaji- "It is a photograph of my only son who was hanged by the Britishers before the war. Perhaps if I had one more son, I would have put him to Madar-e-Hind" as well. Her voice was chocking. She took out the photo from the frame and offered the golden frame on balance.

Subhash babu stood up, touched the feet of the lady and said- "Who says Hindustan won't be independent. The devotion and sacrifices of our mothers, sisters and youth will bring it undoubtedly. "

He addressed to the people standing there- "I am not giving you the message of peace; I am giving you the message to war. You want freedom then prepare yourself for bigger sacrifices, you give me your blood and I shall get you freedom."

The atmosphere felt the words of Byron, the famous English poet. Those words were echoing in the atmosphere.

"Whenever there is a war for freedom,
It won't stop, it brings colors of different shades,
Drenched in blood, the son gets it from his father,
He had passed him the immortal tradition!"

Azad Hind Bank collected more than 20 crores on that day. (1942)

Give me your Blood - I shall get you Freedom

On 24th October 1943 at 12:05 in the night, Netaji declared war against England and America on behalf of the Azad Hind Fauj.

The number of soldiers in Azad Hind Fauj was more than 50000. There were 1500 officers. Membership of the Fauj was more than 1.25 lakhs. 20 lakh people agreed to work according to the order of Azad Hind Fauj.

Netaji used to wear black coat, white pant and black cap. There was magic in his speeches. Everyone used to get charmed and energized whenever he spoke.

One day, he was telling to a crowd- "My sisters and brothers. Our motherland is restless to get freedom but freedom does not come without turmoil. To get it, we have to lost everything. Just forget the days of lavishness and comfort. Freedom seeks sacrifice."

"You give me your blood. I shall get you freedom."

Thousands of people raised their hands, on his call. He said- "Not in this manner, you have to sign the oath-letter with your blood." With this, lots of youth came forward and signed the paper with their blood. Even women also participated actively.

No one had the strength to oppose Netaji. Even Hitler, Mussolini and General Toja would bow down to Netaji.

English spies tried to kill Netaji atleast four times but they didn't succeed. He was a true legend.

★★★

Beaten in Court

When the revolutionaries reached Lahore's Special Magistrate's Court, they were joyful as ever. Bhagat Singh, Rajguru, Sukhdev, Vijay Kumar Sinha, Shiv Verma, Jaidev Kapoor, Kamalnath Tiwari, Dr. Gaya Prasad, Prem Datt, Mahaveer Singh, Batukeshwar Dutt, Jitendra Saniyal, Ajay Ghosh, Sundar Pande, Kishori Lal, Kundan Lal, Deshraj and Atmaram, all were shouting *Vande Mataram* on the way to court. They started singing the song written by Bismil-

"Sarfaroshi ki tamanna ab hamare dil mein hai,
Dekhna hai jor kitna bajuye katil mein hai,
Waqt aane de, bata denge tujhe aye aasman,
Ham abhi se kya bataen, kya hamare dil mein hain,
Aye shaheed-e-mulk-o- millat, main tere upar nisar,
Ab teri himmat ke charche, gair ki mahfil mein hai,
Sarfaroshi ki tamanna ab hamare dil mein hai
Dekhna hai jor kitna bajuye katil mein hai."

Shouting *Inqlaab Jindabad,* they entered the court. After sometime, the traitor and Government's witness Jay Gopal was brought to the court. He was shameless, he looked directly in the eyes of revolutionaries. All rebels started shouting- "Shame! Shame!" Prem Datt was not satisfied with just that. He was short highted. He took out his shoe and threw it towards Jay Gopal. The shoe hit his head. Rajguru said mockingly- "Well shot, my brother! Now another one!!"

Jay Gopal got the second one from Prem Dutt. Other revolutionaries also tried to undo their shoes but they were stopped by the police. The Police tried to handcuff them but they did not allow. There was a chaos in the court room and the court proceeding were adjourned.

Next day, when the revolutionaries were to be taken from Borstal jail to Central jail for Court proceedings, in a truck, they refused. When the police applied force, then revolutionaries also tried their hands on police as their hands were open. Some of them were weak due to hunger strike but Rajguru was in full energy. He fought with police vigorously. Anyhow police controled five of them and loaded them in the truck.

When the truck reached court they assembled at exit door in such a way that no one could pass from that door. That day also the court was adjourned.

Police tricked the revolutionaries, they were told to handcuff themselves and after reaching court they would be released. Revolutionaries agreed that but they were not freed by the police after reaching Court.

At the mid-break, they were given time to have their lunch. Bhagat Singh told police to open their handcuffs while eating food. They had their lunch joyfully and decided not to give chance to police to handcuff them again. When the police came towards them with handcuff, they denied wearing them. The police and the court were already prepared for this. There were many murderers, goons and Pathan present around for different heinous crimes. They were all armed with sticks and were advised to take best care of all the revolutionaries. They were promised with delecious meals of their choice in return of beating the revolutionaries.

They beat up the revolutionaries black and blue, but got resistance from Bhagat Singh and Rajguru. They snatched the sticks and beat up the hooligans furiously with full force. Goons lunged at Bhagat Singh and Rajguru and controlled them. They had been beaten like animals and were left unconscious. Some of the women who came to see the trial screamed with shock and became unconscious.

But the brutal police were not satisfied with the beating in the court. They tortured the revolutionaries even in jail as well. (1930)

★★★

Courage of being someone else's wife

Rash Behari Bose got the courage to orchestrate the revolution from Lahore. He went to Lahore in December 1914. Government was trying its best to capture him. They were afraid of Rash Behari Bose's presence in Lahore. The government issued a circular that one should not give his house to any person who is single. He must be a married person.

Rash Behari had the problem to rent a house without wife and children. Nobody in Lahore was ready to rent him a house. His comrades were also very upset.

A business man named Ramsharan Das, a resident of Lahore, a gentleman and patriot. His wife was also very gentle. When she came to know about the obstacles of getting a rental house for Rash Behari Bose, she solved the problem. She declared herself as wife of Rash Behari Bose and rented a house for them. Bose lived many months with the wife of Ramsharan Das and lived in the same house. This was an example of character and faith of the fight of freedom for the country. That was amazing. It was difficult for a person to leave his wife with someone else like this. He was Ramsharan Das. And who is the person living with someone else's wife without taking any ill advantage of that relation? He was Rash Behari Bose. Rash Behari was revolutionary but also a saint. He had gallantry as well as strong character and faith in his religion.

Rash Behari Bose lived there uptill February 1915. When revolutionary movement failed and many got arrested, then Rash Behari Bose left Lahore secretly and went to Bengal.

★★★

Bravery of Durga Bhabhi

Bhagwati Charan was not in Lahore. He was in Calcutta. He had left 500 rupees with Durga bhabhi and told her to give the money to whoever comes on behalf of Bhagat Singh or Sukhdev. After the killing of Saunders, the money could be used by the revolutionaries to get out of Lahore.

After two days, Sukhdev came and asked Durga bhabhi if she could go out?

"What is the work? Where to go?" She asked.

"We have to take a man out of Lahore. You have to play his wife's role. There is danger their can even be shooting."

Bhabhi agreed. Actually she had to accompany Bhagat Singh to Calcutta.

The train from Lahore to Calcutta was at 6 a.m. Bhagat Singh dressed up like an English *Saheb*. A three years old child of Bhagwati Sharan, Shachi, was with Durga bhabhi as Bhagat Singh wife and child. Rajguru as their servant was in servant's compartment while Bhagat Singh and Durga bhabhi were in first class compartment. Rajguru got down at Lucknow. From Lucknow a telegram was sent to Bhagwaticharan- "Coming with my brother- Durgavati".

It was not clear to Bhagwaticharan who was Durgavati, still he reached station with his elder sister. He felt very delighted to see Sachi and Durga bhabhi with Bhagat Singh.

He appreciated Durga bhabhi and said- "Now, I have understood you". (1930)

★★★

Rani Lakshmi Bai of Jhansi as '*Ranchandi*'

Lakshmibai, the queen of Jhansi, was surrounded by the British Army. She was operating her swords with both the hands. She was like *Ranchandi*, killing the enemy like *Adi-shakti*. Her soldiers saw her fighting like *Bhagwati Durga*. That inspired the soldiers to fight more valiantly.

The battle was at a deciding point. It was the time to save Jhansi from the dirty clutches of Britishers and the Britishers were desperate to take hold of Gwalior.

Sir Hugh Rose was determined to either conquer the Queen or kill himself (do or die) in the battlefield. He was getting news of the queen for every minute. He got the news that the Queen had turned into devil and she was killing the English soldiers brutally with both the hands.

The queen was also searching for Hugh Rose. That's why, she entered into the British troop.

Hugh Rose was standing outside at a distance from his troop. He too was desirous to fight with the Queen.

After all, that opportunity came, when they were face to face. But there was a drain full of water between them. The drain was broad and flowing speedly. The queen tried to made her horse to jump that drain, but that Arbi horse was adamant to cross that drain so it stopped there. Even after repeated efforts, it did not move. By that time, the English soldiers surrounded the queen and she again was fighting with the swords in both her hands. During this fight, one English soldier threw his javelin targeting the back of the queen. She got badly injured. Raghunath Singh and Jawahar Singh were at the back of their queen. Raghunath Singh lifted the queen on his horse, as she was badly injured, and with Jawaharlal Singh and queen, crossed the drain. When Hugh Rose saw the queen, he immedietly rushed towards her, but Raghunath Singh intercepted him. Hugh Rose could not defeat her but Britishers got control over Jhansi.

★★★

Chittagong sets at midnight

On the basis of the trial, Surya Sen and his inmates got death sentence. 12th January 1934 was fixed for execution at 12 o'clock midnight.

The lock of Surya Sen's cell was opened and he had been taken to execution site under tight security. Surya Sen shouted *Vande Mataram* with all his force.

The slogan of *Vande Mataram* echoed throughout the jail and all the prisoners started shouting *Vande Mataram* loudly. They understood that there leader was departing from them.

Jail warden disliked the situation. So, he charged a *lathi* on his head. But Surya Sen was not going to stop. He continued shouting *Vande Mataram* with full force.

He was badly beaten till he became unconscious. Due to the brutality of the jail authority, Suryasen died before hanging. Jail authority became worried due to this incidence but their wisdom worked at the last moment. They took his dead body to the hanging podium and slung the already lifeless body to stage an execution by hanging. Thus set the sun of Chittagong at midnight.

Tarakeshwar Datt was also hanged that night. Britishers carried their bodies and dumped them in a warship before dawn. They were so afraid of Surya Sen and Tarakeshwar Datt as if their spirits would come out and start fighting. Their corpses were drowned in the middle of sea with stones and iron shackles tied to them.

★★★

Brave girls killed the magistrate

The district magistrate of Komilla, Mr. Stevens was an extreme example of brutality. He pledged to kill all the revolutionaries from his district. He used to give painful, severe punishments to the rebels and believed that his cruelty would keep everyone silent and end revolutionary movements. Due to his atrocities, revolutionaries decided to end the district magistrate.

Mr. Stevens was alert about the dangers. He used to go to court very often and worked from home usually. There were many guards in his bungalow. If anyone came to meet him, the guards checked the person thoroughly. One officer was also deputed for his security for 24 hours.

On 14th December 1931 Shanti Ghosh and Sunita Choudhary, the students of class 8th reached his residence in a cart. They told the guard that they wanted to meet Mr. Stevens. One of the girls wrote their names on a slip. But they were different names, Ela Sen and Mira Devi. The slip was sent to the Magistrate. He came out with his SDO and welcomed the girls.

The girls said that they wanted to organise a swimming competition and need help from the Government. They also put up one application to him. The Magistrate took the application and wrote "The principal of the school give her opinion". After writing the comment, he returned the application to one of the girls. The second girl shot two bullets on his chest directly. He tried to run away but fell down. The SDO and guards caught the girls.

Mr. Stevens died on the spot as one bullet hit on his heart. The lawsuit started on Shanti Ghosh and Suniti Chaudhary on 18th January 1932. On 27th January 1932, the decision was declared. Since they were less than 16 years, therefore, they were awarded life imprisonment instead of death sentence.

★★★

Blood for Blood

One of the Revolutionaries of Lahore, Sajjan Singh, was facing a lawsuit for the crime of murder.

Public Prosecutor was questioning Sajjan Singh.

Public Prosecutor: "Mr. Sajjan Singh, you have been charged that you have killed the wife of Captain Curtice; have you killed Mrs. Curtice?"

Sajjan Singh: "I have not killed her, it was just a coincidence."

Public Prosecutor: "Will you tell us how it happened?"

Sajjan Singh: "I went there to kill Captain Curtice not to his wife."

Public Prosecutor: "Then how did that happen?"

Sajjan Singh: "After reaching the bungalow, I wanted to check weather Mr. Curtice was available there or not. I just wanted to check him in the bungalow but his wife didn't allow me. When she violently opposed, I picked her up and threw her. I did not know that she would die due to my act."

Public Prosecutor: "You have injured their two kids also. You do not have any shame harming those small kids?"

Sajjan Singh: "*Janab,* with my 2-3 slaps they were injured only. I just want to ask- What about those children who were killed by gun shots at Jallianwala Bagh? The injured kids crying for water but no one gave them a single drop of water. Did the Brave English soldiers feel shame at that time?"

Public Prosecutor: "I want to ask you why you wanted to kill Mr. Curtice? Any objective behind this?"

Sajjan Singh: "I wanted to take revenge of mass killings at Amritsar and Peshawar, by killing an English officer; that was my only objective.

Public Prosecutor: "You yourself are a military soldier. You should be faithful towards your officers."

Sajjan Singh: "*Janab,* I didn't join Army for salary. I joined it to learn handling and using rifles, and whenever I will get chance, I will shoot any English officer."

Public Prosecutor: "Then you agree that you went to the bungalow of Mr. Curtice to kill him and due to your blow Mrs. Curtice died."

Sajjan Singh: "If taking revenge is a crime then I am admitting my crime."

Sajjan Singh admitted his crime. The Court awarded him death sentence. Before hanging, he shouted *'Shadeed Bhagat Singh Jindabad'*.

Sajjan Singh was a resident of Baltoha village of Lahore district. He was recruited in Punjab Regiment in 1930 and on April 1931 he was hanged.

★★★

Naval Mutiny

In 1945-46, there were revolts by soldiers throughout India. Soldiers were inspired and thrilled by the battle of Azad Hind Fauj. The first revolt took place at Dum Dum Airport, Calcutta, by Air Force. Its affect was spread to other wings. On 18th February 1946, the soldiers of Naval Force started revolting and assaulted English soldiers. The flag of Union Jack was replaced with Congress flag. It was the first incidence happened in the history of Britain. On 19th February 1946, there was an agitation held throughout India supporting soldiers' revolution, A government report was publishcd related to the agitation that there were 18 agitations took place involving 3 lakhs of workers in 1946 in which Government had faced loss of 27,17,000 working hours. Navy soldiers agitated in Mumbai, A huge number of Naval soldiers and local people participated in the procession shouting slogans- *Inquilab Zindabad, Hindustan ko azad karo, Azad Hind Fauj ko azad karo*. There was big clash between English and Indian Naval soldiers. Hundreds of soldiers from both the sides were killed and thousands of people were injured. Although, the Naval force submitted their arms on the request of Sardar Patel, this incident ruined the British reputation.

British Government realised the fact that time has come to leave India. The agitation by Army, Navy and Air Force made them think about the freedom of India. They decided to leave India. After this revolt, British Prime Minister Attlee declared that Pethick Lawrence, Sir Stafford Cripps and A. V. Alexander will come to India and will have a talk with Indian leaders to resolve this issue.

★★★

Gift of four severed heads

Bahadur Shah Zafar was imprisoned with his four sons, Mirza Mughal, Mirza Khijar, Mirza Abu Bakar and Mirza Abdullah. When they reached near the jail the palanquin of Zeenat Mahal changed the direction and the sons were ordered to get down from the cart in other direction. They were tied. Major Hudson himself killed four sons and drank handful of their hot blood. While drinking the blood the princes, he said-

"I was boiling with such a revenge and retaliation that I would be cool only after quanching my such thirst by their blood only."

But he was still bearing the feeling of revenge. He cut the heads of four princes and put them on a tray. He carried the tray to Bahadur Shah and said-

"You are a king, I want to present you a wonderful gift. Plcasc acccpt it."

Bahadur Shah Zafar took the tray with heads in his hands and after a while said- "*Anhmedulillah*! The sons of of Taimur always used to come to their father like this".

By the order of Hudson, their bodies were hanged outside the court and their heads were displayed on Khooni Darwaza in front of the prison.

Mockingly Hudson said to Bahadur Shah Zafar-

"Dumdume main dam nahin, ab khair mango jaan ki,
Ay Zafar, thandi hui ab teg Hindustan ki."

Bahadur Shah felt insulted but replied strongly-

"Gajiyon mein bu rahegi jab tak imaan ki,
Takht-e-London tak legi teg Hindustan ki."

Bahadur Shah was captivated and sent to Burma. On 7th November 1862, the last Mughal emperor of India took his last breath in Rangoon jail.

★★★

Bullet hit- either at back or in chest

When we were a part of the British Kingdom, even small children were aware of freedom.

But the sacrifice made by the youths from Patna had trembled the history. A group of youth in the form of procession reached to the Secretariat. These live narration from "The revolt of 1942" is being presented here.

The procession reached at the Secretariat and everyone was aware of its fate. They were ready for do or die. Who could stop them then. A unique jubilient environment was there. On the other hand, Archer was standing in front of secretariat with Gurkha soldiers. The soldiers were ready with their dangerous rifles.

Mr. Archer shouted- "What do you people want?"

"We want to hoist our flag." One minor student replied.

Irritated Archer said- "Come forward, those who want to hoist the flag."

Suddenly, 11 students came out and stood in a row. Archer asked the little one- "You want to hoist the flag! Ok. But before that remove your shirt."

The boy came forward tore his shirt and stood in front of him with naked chest.

But Archer couldn't telerated this bravery of the child so he ordered to shoot. Within no time, those 11 warriers were killed by soldiers. After that, bullets were coming from rifles like cat and dogs. Many people were killed and some injured but public continued there shouting with slogans- "*Vande Mataram*"; "*Angrejo Bharat Chhodo*". Suddenly, the crowd saw a small lean boy standing on the top of the Secretariat building, carrying the Tricolour and smiling. A huge ocean of the people were seen all around. His sacrifices was successful. The bulshit soldiers had left the place. The Tricolor on the mount of the Secretariat seemed as like waving the fame of those martyrs all around.

6 students were died on the spot only. Others were taken to hospital. One boy was on the operation table, he was unconscious. After sometme when he became conscious, he asked the doctor- "Doctor, where the bullet has hit me, whether in chest or in the back?" Doctor realized his feelings and said- "It's in the middle of your chest." The boy smiled and with pride, he uttered, "Now people won't say that I was hit by bullet if I was running." And , with his last words, he left for heavenly abode. Albeit, the boy is not alive but his supreme sacrifice for the freedom movement of the country has become immortal.

Surprisingly, later the fact came in light that they had fired Dumdum bullets, which were prohibited by the international policy for use, even in war.

★★★

Jailor's cruelty, Soldier's sacrifice

Subhash was shivering with high fever. In a very low and faint voice he said,"water…water"

Jailor came near him, his boots thundered, and with a smile he said- "The God of revolution! You need water. Tell that to your *Vande Mataram*. It will give you water." Subhash was chocking due to thirst. He ignored the mocking way of jailer and kept silent. "Do you understand the result of fighting against British Empire, Mr. Subhash? You still have time, save yourself. Nothing is there in *Vande Mataram*. If you believe then ask water from *Vande Mataram*. I want to see how strong it is," said the jailer, touching his mustache.

Subhash was not able to speak; he was in semi-consciousness state. Maa Durga already came to his vision. The Jailer was continuously making mockery of Subhash. He asked for water from a police constable. When it came, the jailer spilled it on the floor. A few drops fall on Subhash's body too, but he didn't react. He kept quiet.

That police constable could not tolerate the mocking way of jailer. Subhash uttered in a deep faint voice "*Vande Mataram".*

Jailer became furious and mockingly said- "To hell with your Vande Mataram, keep on dying and cry for your Vande Mataram."

The same constable return back with a glass of water and shouted- "You the son of *Laat Saheb,* just see the strength of our revolutionary Netaji". He took Subhash's head on his lap and gave him water. Jailer was shouting and abusing him but the constable did not heed him and after giving water to Subhash, he told in a high tone, "Netaji has high fever, jailer *saheb*."

"So what, you damn fool, you gave him water... I will see you later...". Jailer said angrily.

"Don't use bad words you son of b**! He is our Netaji... he is our lifeline... I kick this filthy cap, belt, medal, uniform, etc." Saying these words, the constable discarded his police uniform.

Subhash witnessed the miraclulous scene. Gradually, he was coming to hid senses. The constable shouted "*Vande Mataram, Netaji Subhash jindabad, Hamari Azadi Amar Rahe.*"

"Just stop... you stupid...", jailer shouted, you have revolted on duty, broken the discipline, you will be punished. Such a punishment so that no one can dare to break descipline."

"Who will punish me? You? You tamed dog!" Constable shouted in a strong voice.

The Constable walked out of the jail. Next day, the news floated that the constable was involved in the conspiracy with revolutionaries and as he ran away from the jail so the police chased him. But despite warning he didn't surrender, ultimately the police shot him. He died. (1931)

★★★

Indigenous sword echoed in England

The History is full of the stories of 1857, the first freedom battle of India. Our soldiers fought bravely with indigenous swords against the modern arms of British. Our fighters had the courage and energy to face rifles, Cannons and other modern arms with javelins and swords. The Britishers were in winning side but they accepted the bravery and spirit of our soldiers. After the battle, so many English officers who went to England wrote their memoirs. One of them was Forbes Michael.

At the time of battle, Forbes Michael was a surgent deputed at Lucknow. When he returned to England he wrote about the swords used by Indian soldiers specifically, particularly on their manufacturing process. It is not only astonaishing but also interesting.

Forbes Michael was incharge of the battle. The fight was face to face and Indian soldiers were killing the British forces rapidly. Britishers were amazed and discussed the matter among them. They understood that their sword work was useless in comparison to the Indians. At that time, the swords made in Berkingham were supposed to be best. Forbes Michael wrote some amazing incidents he witnessed.

When the fight was going on, one Indian soldier struck the head of a British soldier James Reddy with a sword and the head was broken into two pieces. Then by second stroke the body was separated from head. Two brothers of James were in the same battlefield. One brother of James, John saw his brother's killing, furiously he came close to the Indian soldier. Blew the bonet of his rifle on the soldier, but before falling the soldier struck his sword on John's shoulder and the body of John was devided into two pieces. The third brother also came and lifted the sword of the Indian soldier who was dead by that time and cut soldiers head from his body.

The English officers curiously examined the swords of Indian soldiers. They came to know that before using the sword in battlefield, Indians test the sword in a unique way.

They used to keep a big fish surrounded by cotton and placed it on a cot. If the fish cut into two pieces by one stroke the sword was permitted to use in fight. For the sharpness of sword, it was dipped in arsenic solution.

Forbes Michael even suggested British officers to improve their own swords that were made in England and should make new swords by keeping the Indian swords as reference model.

★★★

Cell of 2½ × 2½ for a Man of 6¼

A special punishment was given to rebel Sardar Bhan Singh in the prison of Andaman. He was dumped into a cell of 2 and half by 2 and half. He was 6 feet and a quarter inches tall, much big for such a small space. His crime was that he used to sing patriotic songs all the time and would not stop singing for any one.

Bhan Singh was a resident of Sunet village in Ludhiana district of Punjab. He joined Army, then left the job and went to America. Then he joined Gadar Party. With the first group of the members of Gadar Party, he came by 'Korea' ship, he reached India. All the way, he used to sing patriotic songs and wherever the ship stopped he told others that they were going to free their Nation by fighting Britishers. On 29th October 1914, he landed in Calcutta but got arrested by the police. For few days, he was in Montgomery jail but was released after sometime. Meanwhile, he started participating actively in Gadar Party. Again arrested, case was filed but he got the punishment for life and thrown away to Kalapani, Andaman Jail.

Initially, he was kept in a big cell on ground floor but when he argued with jail officers and shifted to second floor in another cell with sackles in his arms and legs. He could not tolerate wrong things going on in jail and very often he used to quarrel with the officials. He got severe punishments. The amount of his meal and water was reduced to half. He was big built man and needed more food and water.

But still he never stopped his singing in full volume. Jail officials had to stop him but could not succeed. Out of frustration, he was thrown into a small cell of two and half by two and half feet on the 3rd floor. He was not able to sit or sleep. Sometimes,

he spent his whole night standing and slept there for few hours.

One day, the jail Superintendent came for inspection. Again, he argued with the officer. The officer abused him using filthy words. Bhan Singh roared like a lion and scolded the officer. The superintendent had such experience for the first time. Out of humiliation and frustration, he called 10 to 12 prisoners and instructed them to attack on Bhan Singh. He fought courageously but the brutal prisoners broke his bones. He started vomiting blood too. He was hospitalised but after some days the freedom lover, and the singer of patriotic songs died there. (1919)

★★★

Rajguru's Trial by Fire

The Revolutionaries rented a house at Agra. They used to organise their meetings and discuss on next plannings etc. in that house. Everything was secret. In 1928, one day bhaiya (Chandrashekhar Azad) was explaining the different methods used by the police and CID to take out the informations from the rebels. He said- "Sometimes the pain of torture becomes so intolerable that the person is compelled to utter some secrets about their group. So it is better not to become a victim in police hands. If you don't get any way to escape, then it would be better to fight back and sacrifice your life." The gathering was keenly listening to Azad.

The revolutionaries used to do their daily household work by themselves turn by turn. That day Rajguru was making chapatis. He was also listening carefully the suggestions of Azad. He was moved by the thoughts. Suddenly he thought he was losing his self-confidence. Immediately he decided to take a test of his own confidence. He put the pot holder inside the oven and heated it till red. He put that red hot iron pot holder on his chest. The skin burnt due to heat. He repeated the act 7 times and kept silent. His friends did not know about it.

At night, Azad could hear the moans Rajguru made while sleeping in pain. He saw Rajguru was sleeping but his hands were on his chest. Azad woke him up and asked the reason. At first Rajguru denied anything but ultimately narrated everything to Azad whatever he did and why.

"Oh my God! What you have done!" Azad was in tremendous shock. He had tears in his eyes and said- "I told all these as general information for everyone and you took it personally".

Rajguru was speechless. He had seen the tears in the eyes of Azad, and the love, affection made him more confident and determined.

Immedietly Azad opened his shirt and saw the seven erupted blisters on the skin. He applied some homemade medicine on them. What more they could have done for treatment at midnight. (1929)

★★★

Role of labourers in freedom struggle

Lokmanya Bal Gangadhar Tilak, Lala Lajpat Rai and other veteran leaders tried to unite the workforce of India to have their participation in freedom fight after First World War.

In 1908, almost 1.5 Lakh workers agitated for 6 days after the arrest of Lokmanya Tilak. He was arrested and sent to Mandalay Central Jail. That was the first political agitation by the workers.

Before that, in 1905, the government printing press workers denied to publish gadget in which the Division of Bengal was notified.

From 1918 to 1920, the workforce of different places agitated several times as the price of daily essential comodities had been increased but they kept getting the same wages. In 1920, approximately 15 lakh work force agitated.

In November 1921, the Prince of Wales was welcomed with strikes and agitation by the workers in Mumbai. That resulted into a fight and the State Army was deputed to control the situation. So many workers died at that time.

In 1927, the workers started May Day celebration at commercial centres. Although in 1923, May Day was celebrated in Madras by Singaravelu Chettiar.

In 1925, the textile workers went on strike opposing increase in production and tax deduction from wages. The rules were abolished for the time being. The strike was supported by the work force of England, Soviet Union and Germany.

In 1930, 50000 workers of textile mills stopped against the arrest of Gandhiji at Solapur. Along with the public support, they took control of the city and established their own governance. British administration ordered Marshal Law and brutally

suppressed the agitation. Four workers were hanged publicly.

In 1934, workers went on to strike against rationalisation, cutting of wages and retrenchment. Despite the trade unions suppression, time to time, by the Britishers, the agitations continued and progressed.

On September 1939, the Second World War started. The viceroy also declared India's participation. Workers of Mumbai, approximately 90000 of them, declared strike against imperialiastic war on 2nd October 1939.

There were several strikes for dearness allowance and war bonus, as the prices of commodities were rising high due to war.

In 1946, the Indian Naval Force which was under Britishers revolted and captured the ports. Approximately 3 lakh workers went on strike. British Government fired at the workers on strike. As per Government record, 250 people died, but according to non official sources it was more than 400.

The workers played a vital role in the Freedom Movement, which impacted the the programmes or movements related to the Indian freedom struggle.

★★★

Tore saree to hoist the flag

The fight for freedom witnessed not just the participation from men but women members were took an active part in it as well. In the book *"Anand Math"* written by Bankim Chandra, at one place Swami Satyanand told that "In Anand Math, women are not allowed because their devotion towards revolution is doubtful".

The reply is also in the same book through the speech of Mahamaya- "to sacrifice for motherland is not the right of men only, women could also perform the important role".

Many women, who were the supporter of freedom fight, supported her. There were lots of women revolutionaries in the history of freedom fight. Madam Bhikaji Cama was one of them. No one could imagine that a girl from well-to-do Parsi family would fight for freedom from outside the country.

Madam Cama was born on 24th September, 1861, in Mumbai. She was one of the nine children of Sodab Ji Patel. Her father got admitted her in an English School with an intention that she should be brought up in the western culture. But she was a true daughter of *Bharat Mata* and always felt sorry to see the discrimination of Indian people.

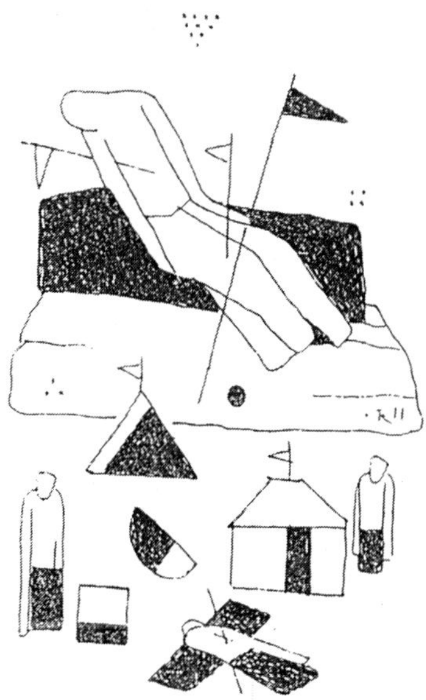

In 1885, when the Congress got established, she joined the party and became its active member and with full devotion, she started doing beneficial work for the upliftment of the women of all the sections of the society.

She was married at an early age, but that didn't cause any hindrance in her work. She started touring foreign countries. In 1905, she went to London. The honorable leader and freedom fighter Dadabhai Naroji was in London at that time. She worked as a secretary to him for one and half years.

In 1907, she participated in International Socialist Federation at Stuttgart in Germany and hoisted the first Indian National Flag. While hoisting the flag she said- "It is a tradition of my country, to spesk under the flag. But I am sorry; I don't have my country's flag with me. But it did not matter." She was very excited and ripped apart her colourful and beautiful saree and waved it like an Indian flag. Then she said- "It is my national flag, have salutaion to it." The whole gathering claped and shouted- "Long Live India!" Matching the sound of slogans, Madam Cama raised her voice and said- "Wake up Indians! Hold your head high and stand straight against the atrocity."

Madam Cama will always be remembered for her devotion to her motherland. She died in August 1937 at Mumbai.

★★★

Mahavir Singh was *'Mahavir', in true sense*

One incident of the Bellary jail was spread far off places, when Mahavir Singh knocked down the Jail Suprintendent, who was a boxer, to earth, with a single hit only. It was a terrible hit and could not bore the same. From that day onwards, he never dare to do boxing with any prisnor. But the superintendent could not digest the insult; so why did he leave Mahaveer Singh with any punishment. So, he anounced a punishment of 30 lashes of whip to Mahaveer.

Preparations were going on in Bellary jail for the punishment. Whip (Cane) was soaked in water. A robust prisnor was chosen to hit that whip Mahaveer. He was given win and was told to rip the skin and flesh out of the body of Mahavir Singh. If he failed, he would be punished in the same manner. But if he could do it properly, he would be rewarded. Mahavir Singh was brought out of his cell.

Mahavir Singh was laied on a tipoy. The three legs of the tipoy were inserted firmly in the ground. Hands and legs of Mahavir were tied. He was undressed and his waist was tied with a belt to the tipoy.

Jail Superintendent reached the spot to have the pleasure with his team. The main warden looked at the jail suprintendent to seek his nod, so that could start doing the same. He ordered the warden to proceed. Then, the warden further gave ordered to the concern prisnor who was deputed for the same task.

The prisnor took the wet whip and flung it in the air. A sound cracked in the air. He took two steps back and hit the Mahavir's naked body. With the first lash of the whip, the skin ripped open and blood oozed out from the Mahavir's body, and few drops of blood too fell on the ground. After that , he didn't bother where to hit and started whipping blindly. Blood started flowing like a stream on the ground. It all became red. With every slash, Mahavir shouted *Inquilab Zindabad* excitedly. 30 lashes completed, then Mahaveer was untied. A stretcher was ready there to take him to his cell but he kicked the stretcher and walked towards his cell.

Jail Suprintendent was surprised. He thought that this prisoner was one of the unique pieces, what if every prisoner could become Mahavir Singh, then how he would surely lose his job!

The Government decided to shift Mahaveer Singh to Kala Pani in Andaman, to make such stubborn prisoners to settle down their mind.

In January 1933, some selected revolutionaries were sent to *Kala Pani,* Andman. Total 84 revolutionaries from Bengal, Bihar, Uttar Pradsh and Punjab were setteled in the cells of Andman.

★★★

Detached neck from body, with shovel

Rohini Barua was given so much of atrocities in the jail, for, he decided why not to do suicide. But that thought couldn't stand in his mind. Rather, he determined to kill the person who had imprisoned him on the basis of doubt only. Though he didn't commit any wrongdoing. Moreover, he was kept in such a dirty dungeon place where nobody stands even for a while. And tortured brutally.

Those police personnel, who were infamous for torturing of revolutionaried, Syed Irshad Ali was one of them who was well known for oppressing the revolutionaries and he was the person who arrested Rohini and forced him to stay in a dirty cell. He was fond of finding new methods to torture Barua. Irshad Ali was famous for his cruelty with revolutionary. He was charge of Gwalanda police station in Faridpur. He arrested 18 years old Rohini only on the basis of doubts and his tortures were increasing day by day.

In the meantime, Rohini's mother died. Rohini was not allowed to go home and his relatives were also denied from meeting him. Rohini's brother's wife also died after sometime but Irshad Ali did not give him permission to go home. Rohini became frustrated.

One day, the station incharge was giving instructions to all the jail mates to clean the ground. He gave a shovel to Rohini to lift soil here and there. Rohini got a chance to utillize it in a better way. He struck the shovel on the neck of Irshad Ali thrice with full force. The head of Irshad Ali was separated from his body. Everyone in the jail was happy with this act because he was a cruel man. It happened at 8 a.m. on the 15th June 1935. Irshad Ali could survive for a short while.

The lawsuit presented before the Special Tribunal. On the 18th December 1935, Rohini Barua was hanged in Faridpur jail. The irony is that even his dead body was not handed over to his relatives.

★★★

Tied rifle & pistol to sister's legs

Ram Prasad Bismil and Ashfaq-Ullah Khan had problem to carry the guns and rifles to Shahjahanpur from Gwalior. There was a strict vigilance by police officers on the way. Bismil had an idea; he alone went to Shahjahanpur and brought his younger sister Shastri Devi with him.

Ram Prasad tied the rifle and pistol & rivolver to the legs of his sister and covered them with bandage as if the legs were injured and broken. Ashfaq and Bismil carried Shastri Devi by their hands and laid her on a berth. On the way, they replied the queries that she fell down from a height and broken her legs. After getting First aid here, now they were taking her to Lucknow for better treatment. In this way, by playing such a trick, they succeeded to come back to Shahjahanpur with the arms. (1925)

★★★

Catching him was Tough-Nut-To-Crack

A crowd was reading a paper pasted on the wall of the office of Assistant Station Master at Lahore. Just then Rash Behari Bose reached there. He was dressed like a Punjabi with turban on his head. He stopped there to see what the crowd was seeing. He tried to move at front by making way for him. For this, a few persons objected too for his such a behaviour. He told the crowd like a proper Punjabi and in the same tone to let him also see what everyone was seeing so eagerly for long.

He was astonished, when Rash Behari saw his own photo along with a poster pasted on the wall, in that 12000 rupees reward was declared who will catch him. Below his pic, his personality was also briefed as-

"A tall man, strong body, big eyes, clean shaven, the third finger of his hand is stiff and with a scar, approx. 30 years old. The offender dresses like a bengali, punjabi or sometimes even sage's dress. He generally travels to Rawalpindi, Gurdaspur, Ferozepur, Jhelam and Lahore. Search him especially in Bengali colonies, Kali temples, or Hindu's Shivalaya. Also search hin in all Dharamshala, Sarai and Railway stations.

Watching and reading his own description amongst public, Rash Behari Bose neither astonished nor he tried to get escape from there; instead he spoke in Punjabi in a calm manner- "*Badshaho*!! If I catch this man, I will be realaxed. I will kick my job and settle at Lahore with 12000 rupees and start some business. Don't you think, *Badshado!* Is it fine?"

Crowd had a mixed reaction-

"It is not easy to catch him. He always keeps bomb and pistol with him".

"To whom, the police even failed to catch him, then how can a common man catch him?"

"This man is very clever and alert. He changes his dresses frequently and get adjusted accordingly, always in disguise, and can speak many languages fluently".

After sometime, the British government came to know that Rash Behari Bose had fled from India and reached Japan. Then the Government deputed a very senior Intelligence official, D. Pitree, to arrest Bose in 1916 and sent him to Japan. Even after relentless chase, the official could not catch Rash Behari Bose.

British government was afraid of the activities of Rash Behari Bose and planned different ways to either kill or kidnap him in Japan. But Bose cheated English detectives and Japanese police. It needs to be mentioned here that Mr. M.Toyama, a Japanese military man gave protection to Rash Behari Bose. And , a Japanese couple, Mr. M. Agisoma and Mrs. Cocco Soma, loved him like their own child and provided full protection. The couple was so impressed with Rash Behari Bose that they arranged marriage of Rash Behari Bose with their daughter Toshiko in 1918. Rash Behari Bose and Toshiko had one son and a daughter.

★★★

He never dare to call Hindustanis as 'Dog'

In the black cells of Andaman Jail, some of the resilient revolutionaries were punished with 30 lashes of whip. The prisoners were restless, especially those who had not faced that punishment. The whip started lashing at the revolutionaries. The inmated were worried and had mixed responses-

"I think everybody will shout and cry."

"I want to see Pandit Parmanand ji, how he faces the punishment! A robust and terrible executioner has been called for him and alcohol will also be offered to him."

"Yes, it's true. Pandit ji will surely be thrashed badly, as jailer Barry is very furious with him. He will surely take revenge of his insult."

"Whatever revenge he will take but Pandit ji has taught him a good lesson. Barry will never forget his insult by Pandit ji, but

he will certainly forget to call any Hindustani, a dog."

"Yes! Despite Pandit Ji's handcuffed hands and legs, he fought with the jailer and taught him a good lesson. Had he been free on that day, he would have killed the jailer."

"Despite his handcuffs, he hit on his head so forcefully that Jailer Barry knocked down."

"With his handcuffed hands, how he catch hold his hair and tharashed him on ground 2-3 times."

"Now that English man, at least, won't dare to fight with Pandit ji again."

"He won't dare to fight with Pandit ji. But will always try to torture him."

And truly, the Jailer ordered a terrible punishment for Pandit Parmanand. Firstly he was to be lashed 30 whips. Then, Pandit ji was brought to the site of punishment. He was stripped naked. The warden tied his hands and legs to a strong tipoy. Especially called, the robust executioner came and started slashing whip on Parmanand's naked body. Everyone was expecting that Pandit Ji would cry out but he was determined not to break his silence. Jailer Barry got furious; he took the whip from the executioner and lashed the whip forcefully on Panditji. But Pandit Ji was determined not to show any sort of weakness. After sometime, jailer got tired. He again handed over the whip to the executioner. After that, the executioner terribly started lashing the whip on Pandit Ji's body. and completed 30 lashes. Due to lashes, Pandit ji was badly hurt, his skin was oozing blood too. When pandit ji was getting untied from tipoy, the jailer was standing far for his security. Pandit Ji stared him and warned- "Now if you come into my grip, I won't let you go alive".

Generally what happened, when any prisoner was lashed off, after that jail staff used to bring a stretcher and take him back to his cell, as the prisoner used to become unconscious after that. Thus a stretcher was brought for Pandit Ji also, but he looked at with hate and climbed the stairs himself to reach his cell. All the revolutionaries were felt very proud of him.

After that incident, the jail officials were keeping distance from him and the jail staff started giving him more facilities. His bravery made stories everywhere. (1915)

★★★

Need brave soldiers... Salary:Death; Pension:Freedom

The people of Gadar Party published in their weekly magazine "Gadar" that within no time there will be a World War and England will be busy with war. So, Indian people should prepare themselves to fight against the British for freedom; it is an opportunity before Indians.

The World War started before their assumed time. The Gadar Party engaged itself in the preparation for going to India to participate in the fight.

They published an advertisement in their weekly magazine-

"Needed brave soldiers to start Gadar in India."

Salary : Death

Reward : Martyrdom

Pension : Freedom

Place of War : India

This advertisement had a very positive impact. All the Indians living outside the country like America, Canada were anxious to sacrifise themselves for the freedom of their country. Thousands of people boarded ships and reached India. With the help of German High Commission, which was situated in America, they were getting arms. They were over enthusiastic, so could not control their emotions. They used to declare everywhere that they were going to India to fight Britishers and get our freedom. For, the British detectives used to inform British Indian Government about their movements and information. Because of that, they suffered many difficulties, and on reaching India they were arrested by the British police. (1919)

★★★

Offered chopped hand to Ma Ganga

It was Kunwar Singh who fought for freedom at the age of 80. He proved that for a brave man freedom of his country is supreme and if needed age is not a factor.

He was master of gorilla warfare. In 1857, like thunderstorm he killed several English enemies with his sword and his bravery dazzles the pages of history. To describe his skills in war, Savarkar wrote in his book 'Indian Freedom Battle of 1857'-

"In Gorilla warfare, no one could match the strategies and skills of Kunwar Singh. After Shivaji, he was the person who proved its importance in war. He was the person who knew all skillful conducts and approaches of gorilla warfare."

The English Soldier could not understand the techniques of his fight. Sometimes he pushed them, sometimes attacked them from sides or sometimes directly hit them. He made soldiers mad by his unique skills and before they assumed the direction, he attacked them from somewhere else.

Kunwar Singh and his Battalion had to cross Ganga River. English soldiers were behind them. Kunwar Singh tried a trick; he spread a rumour that they were crossing the river from Ballia with the help of elephants. English commander Douglas reached near the bank of Ganga in Ballia. Kunwar Singh was in Shivrajpur and started crossing the river by boat.

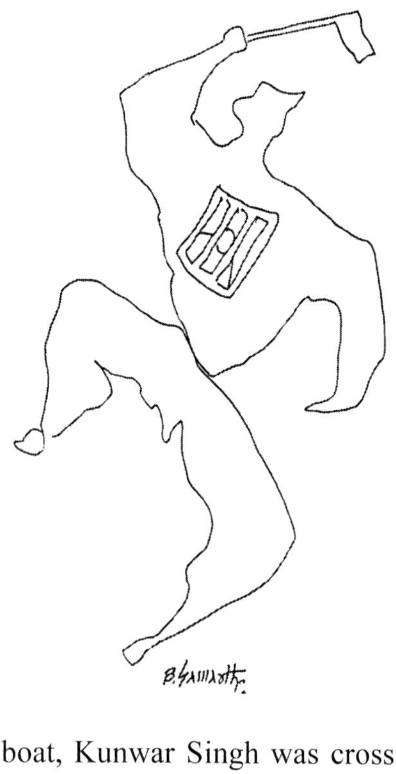

Shivrajpur is 7 miles from Ballia. When Douglas came to know about it, he rushed towards Shivrajpur. By that time, the whole Battalion of Kunwar Singh had already crossed the river. In the last boat, Kunwar Singh was crossing the river. Douglas reached there and started firing on him. One bullet penetrated the left hand of Kunwar Singh. Kunwar Singh thought about spreading of the poison in blood through bullet, he cut his own left arm from elbow by his right hand with his sword. Kunwar Singh dedicated his hand to Ganga with full devotion. He was such a great fighter. (1858)

★★★

First martyr of freedom struggle

The hilly area of Bihar (now in Jharkhand) witnessed a big fight between the native Santhal people and English Army. The intention of the English Army was to capture the whole hilly area which belonged to Santhalies; while Santhal people were fighting to save their land from English. The leader of Santhali Rebels Tilka Manjhi and British Army was under Magistrate Mr. Clevland.

Tilka was sitting on the top of a palm tree to watch how far the English Army were. Mr. Clevland spotted Tilka on the top of the tree. He took the opportunity and went under the tree with an intention to capture Tilka Manjhi dead or alive. He called for his troop to follow him.

Under the palm tree, he askled Tilka to drop his arrow and bow and surrender before him. Tilka was a great fighter. He tied his legs to the trunk of the tree, freed his hands and aimed his arrow towards Clevland. The arrow penetrated his chest. He fell down from the horse. Tilka quickly came down the tree, and before English troops could reach the spot, he ran away and merged into the forest. When English troops reached there, Clevland was already dead.

Tilkamanjhi was a master of gorilla warfare. He and his friends fought furiously in Munger, Bhagalpur and throughout Santhal Parganas with English Army.

Under the leadership of Sir Arthur Koot, Britishers made a plan to catch Tilka. The English Army stopped chasing the Santhalis for a few days. Tilka thought that they had accepted the defeat and went away from their land. All Santhalis rebels started celebrating their victory. One night, they were celebrating the victory with dance, songs and fervour; when they were busy in their merriment, the English Army, which hid themselves, suddenly attacked them. The attack was virocious. Many Santhali soldiers died and some of them were caught by the Britishers. Tilka Manjhi escaped and later continued his fight from different parts of hills and forests.

One day, Tilka and his soldiers attacked on English troop. They were determined to eliminate the Army completely. It was a horrific battle. Santhal rebels killed many English soldiers but at last English Army captured Tilka.

To take revenge show of their defeats and losses, the EnglishArmy hangd him on a banyan tree publicly. He is no doubt the first martyr who fought against the Britishers for freedom of country. After 90 years of his sacrifice, the first freedom fight started in 1857. (1967)

★★★

Jumped from 1st floor in the backyard

Majumdar and Bagchi became close friends. As their thoughts, actions and passion were of same wavelength. They became friends like two bodies one soul.

They chose Guwahati as the centre of their activities. Although they had no permanent address, they travelled to Dhaka or Assam and other places frequently so that Police could not get them.

They established two houses as centers in Assam. Both were not far away. One was near Atgaon jail and the other one in Fancy Bazar. On 7th January 1918, Police attacked their Atgaon residence. They had a fight with police. Both sides fired at each other. Till their guns were loaded, revolutionaries did not allow anyone come close. When all the bullets were finished, they were succeeded to run away from there.

From Atgaon, both the friends reached their second house 'Navagriha'; but sniffer dogs in the British CID have sharp smelling sense, they searched out their presence in that house. It was lunch time, and might be the dogs would have smelled food too, it was 2 p.m. The revolutionaries were busy taking lunch. Police attacked the house suddenly. They fired with their pistols; injured some of the police persons and they again escaped from there. It was 10th January 1918; the police got frustrated due to repeated failure. The life of any revolutionary is always at stake. And, police always keep vigil on them.

Once in 1916, Tarini Prasanna Majumdar was surrounded by the police force within his house at Bhawanipur, district Comilla. Majumdar was on rooftop. He jumped from the first floor in the backyard of the house. His one leg was injured. At the back gate, the police force was deployed. To save himself; he tore his clothes. He took the disguise of a beggar and slowly limped out of the gate. It was a dare task to come out amongst the police. Had the police have doubt and come to know then anything could have done to him. One can only think about this.Majumdar was a witty revolutionary. He didn't fear at any situation or difficulty. If he got a bit scared, then the police perhaps broke his another leg too.

This entire time police failed to catch them. Police got more determine and vigilant. Majumdar and Bagchi, with other revolutionary friends were chased everywhere by police, it was impossible for them to hide and run. One day police got information that they were in a house at Kalta Bazar in Dhaka. Then and there, Police took a huge force and surrounded the house. On 15th January 1918, the revolutionaries were caught from the house. It was impossible for three revolutionaries to fight with 30 policemen. Or for how long.

★★★

Matangini Hajra- A Flame of Revolution

On 29th September 1942, a big incident happened. The revolutionaries decided to attack the police station, court, Government offices; collectively at the same time. To make it happened, lots of trees were cut to block the roads, 30 bridges were destroyed, telephone & telegraph wires were cut down; more than 200 poles were broken down. The stilled boats on the rivers of Kosi and Hooghly were drowned in the river. In those plannings, an old leader Matangini Hazra of that region also played an inportant role. She was a veteran leader and had great influence there.

As per planning, around 3 p.m., approximately one lakh people, divided into 5 groups, from 5 directions took processions to the main police station of Tamluk. The procession which was coming from North side was lead by 73 years old lady Matangini Hazra herself. Processions were being stopped on way as British police came to know about the agitation at night only so their army cleaned all the roads and by 2 p.m. British police prepared themselves accordingly.

The fight was tough. Firstly, the procession of Matangini Hazra was stopped at Vanpukur, and police started lathi charging on 5000 people who were in the procession. Near Diwani Court, police started firing. One boy was killed in that firing. The crowd stopped for sometime but the shout of 'Do or Die' by Matangini Hazra encouraged them with new energy. She, with the tricolour in her hand shouted *Vande Mataram* and in her speech, asking the Indian soldiers to leave the British employment. The second

bullet shot at her one hand and the third one at her another hand. She was injured but held the flag high. Meanwhile, a bullet penetrated her head and she fell down. But she didn't leave the tricolor, it was still in her old hands. Then the fourth bulled hit her on her forehead, and she fell down immedietely. The tricolor was still in her hand. The flag fell down only when one soldier came and kicked at her hands.

But then, a little boy of 14 years came and held the flag up. Soon he toowas killed as well. Turn by turn people came and held the tricolour high and got killed. The number of martyrs started increasing and the injured persons were countless.

★★★

Tricolour flag, ready overnight, by tearing sarees

In 1930, on the day of Salt Satyagrah (Dandi March); with few volunteers, one young lady reached the Bombay Stock Exchange area. She had small packets of illegal salt. She was selling them among the people in the name of freedom and collected almost 40000 rupees within an hour. It was illegal;

hence police arrested her as the leader of the group. She was presented at the court. Even there, she sold so many packets in the presence of the Magistrate. The Magistrate was surprised by the courage of this young girl. She stood on witness box and the Magistrate asked her about her actions. She replied with full confidence and in loud voice- "You are asking me why I sold those packets! I am asking you- why are you involved in this sin? Why don't you leave the job and come with Indians?" She was imprisoned for 9 months. The lady was Kamla Devi. Later, she became internationally famous as Kamla Devi Chattopadhyay.

One more interesting event about her-

There was an International Women Federation in Berlin. Kamla Devi was the leader of Indian representatives. Every country had their flag in the Federation but as India was not a free country, Union Jack was selected for Indians. She shouted in the meeting that if we could not hoist our own flag, we would not participate. The president of the Federation did not know the fact that India had no flag of their own. She said, "Bring your national flag, we have no problem to hoist it." but it was impossible to bring the flag from India. Kamla ji prepared the flag with her saree and next day she entered the venue with our own flag.

Kamla Devi was like a guest to jail. It was not easy to spend time in jail for women freedom fighters. She was released and once again did something anti British and was sent to jail again. She continued her jail journey from 1930 to 1944. She always got pleasure by breaking the laws of Britishers as well as the unhealthy laws of the society made against women. To give training to women workers, she was selected by National Congress. That is why she was always seen standing in front of all the striked and movements pursued by ladies.

The sacrificing story of Preetilata-

Surya Sen had planned to take revenge of the killings of his friends (revolutionaries). He planned to kill the English people going to the European Club for entertainment at the foofhill of a hill. He suggested Preetilata as leader of a group of revolutionaries to conduct the mission. He had seen the courage and energy of that girl. He said to Preetilata- "Listen sister! Arrest or torture by police is bitter, better we die before that. If you don't get time to save yourself from the struggle, have poison and drink that". This was the last suggestion given by Surya Sen to his faithful follower.

On 24th of September 1932, Kalpana Dutta gave potassium cyanide to Preetilata in a pouch. Preetilata kept it in her pocket and dressed with pistols and bombs. She started her journey towards the club. The Englishmen were drunk and entertaining themselves with dance and songs. After reaching the main gate of the club, Preetilata ordered her mates- "Dear friends! Move forward quitely. No English man should go alive from here." Then the bombings and firing was started by the revolutionaries. The music inside changed into the sound of cry and shouting. One English woman died. Thirteen got injured. Some ran away, some tried to resist the fight. In that commotion, one bullet penetrated Preetilata. She was firing as well as running from the site. But British people were chasing her and blood was oozing from the scar. She thought, now the time has come for martyrdom. Also, she thought that rather to be badly treated bt the Britishers, it would be better to die. Then she thought about the pouch that she carried along with her. She rememberd what she was told by Surya Sen; she opened the pouch and took the cyanide capsule in her mouth and martyred for our country.

She was only 17 years old. The tender age of youth; to be in love, happy and joyful. She played with bullets. At the age of enjoying mehendi ceremony etc. she chose pistols and moved on the way of the freedom of our Motherland. She is compared with Rani Lakshmi Bai (martyr of 1857 rebellious movement for the freedom of our Motherland) who never faced defeat. She was the first lady to prefer death before being arrested. She challenged Britishers with arms and fought like Lakshmi Bai till her death without surrendering. She was a true martyr.

★★★

Extreme bravery despite no palm and fingers

Martyr Sufi Amba Prasad had only one hand. Like him, Charu Chandra had his hands but the right hand had no palm or fingers. But both were Patriots. They lived and died for the country.

After his studies, Charu became a worker in a printing press called '*Hiteshi*,' in Howrah, Bengal. He had a thin and short body. No one could imagine that he was a revolutionary. He had strong will power. He was a member of Revolutionary Party.

Whenever he thought about his shortcomings, he consoled himself that for a courageous person- "One hand is enough, what is the use of two hands if one does not have courage."

He was only 18 years old and no one knew his background or could guess his status.

Ashutosh Bishwas was a Government lawyer at Alipur Court. He was famous for his misdeeds. He was always extra strict with revolutionaries. He could convert a right case into wrong and always try to give hardest possible punishment to revolutionaries. All the revolutionaries hated him and wished

to kill him or make him handicapped. But ultimately they planned to kill him.

Charu took the task. Some of his friends had doubt on him because of his crippled hand. But Charu told them not to worry. He said- "Let me show you the wonders I can do with my crippled hand. It will be as effective as the hands of a normal person. Give me a chance to show the utility of my arm." He went to Alipur jail to inspect the activities and whereabouts of Ashutosh Biswas. Biswas was government lawyer; he used to come daily to the court. One day, Charu went there prepared but could not get chance to kill him. Charu was waiting for a perfect moment.

On 10th February 1909, Charu went to court with full preparation. He saw Biswas running around, busy with cases. Charu decided to finish the job that day.

In the evening, around 4 o'clock, Biswas left the court from Eastern side and moved towards the Western side. A sound of gun shot was heard. The bullet penetrated the body of Bishwas and he ran towards Southern side of the court. Charu chased him like a lion and again fired a bullet. Bullet went through Bishwas' body. He entered the room of Court Inspector and died there.

Police came from the back and caught Charu. Before they could catch him, one more fire was shot but it missed the target. Police snatched the revolver. They were surprised, the revolver was tied to the incomplete right hand with a strap and a rope was hanging from it. By pulling the rope with left hand the trigger was pressed!

Charu was beaten severely by police. They asked him about his other inmated but Charu kept silent. He lied to them about a person Pancholi Charu who lived in Dhaka. Police searched everywhere but did not get any clue. After all, Charu was a revolutionary not an informer.

★★★

Spark ignited for the freedom of India

The fire of dissatisfaction was again set due to the atrocities and provocation of English inside the kingdom. Gradually, it took the shape of revolt against British. General Tikendra Jeet Singh became restless and in September 1890, he revolted against the English Government. The English Government was not prepared and their army was defeated. But the Government decided to punish the king and suppress the revolt. They gathered huge army.

In March 1891, the English Army surrounded the Manipur Fort and warned the king that they should drop the arms, surrender, and take shelter under British Government. The king felt insulted as his ego was hurt. He denied. But he agreed to talk to three Generals of English Army to settle the matter. English Army was pleased and thought the king would agree with them.

They prepared a draft in which submission of the kingdom to English Government was declared.

The paper turned out to be a warrant for 3 generals. As they entered the Fort, they were caught and killed at once. When English Army got the news they were alarmed. One night, the English Army attacked Manipur Fort. It was midnight, but the king was prepared for such situation. There was a big fight between King's Army and English Army. The English Army was defeated and they ran away from there.

But Britishers were determined to establish their kingdom in India; they started working on different strategies. They collected huge army and again attacked Manipur. There was fierce battle between the two Armies. Again, the British Army was defeated. Repeated victory made public joyous and they regarded their king undefeatable. English government became more furious with repeated defeat.

Next time, their preparation was strong, they arranged heavy cannons from Burma and skilled force. They attacked Manipur Fort with heavy cannon. King did not have such cannons. The walls of fort broke due to thundering strokes of cannons. It was not safe to stay in the fort, the king left the fort. The Army was disappointed without their king. The Army felt insecured. Unfortunately, General Thingal of King's Army and King's younger brother Egnis Sen were caught by the English Army.

Now, the search started for king. He was hiding inside his kingdom. English people bribed the local and got the information about the king. English Army surrounded King Tikendrajeet Singh, he had a few soldiers who fought bravely but ultimately, he was arrested by the English Army. Manipur came under the control of English.

English were eager to take revenge of their three generals. They did not kill king Tikendrajeet Singh, his younger brother Egnis Sen and General Thingal directly and immediately. They arranged a mocking court and put the prisoners on trial. The allegation on the prisoners was to revolt against British Kingdom and conspiracy against English Government and to throw away English people from India. As usual, the result of revolt was death. On 13th August 1891, three brave people were hanged at Kaithal Achoba publicly.

In the name of justice, English people played a dirty game and Manipur came under British Kingdom. As the last flame of revolution that rose in 1890-91 at Manipur was extinguished. But like this, there were many such flames that erupted everywhere in India and lastly on 15th August 1947 burnt the rule of British Kingdom forever. Long live our Freedom; long live our Free India!

★★★

Completed the task by shooting in court

It was a challenge before Sikh community to punish the person who killed Sardar Bhag Singh and Sardar Vatan Singh. Also the person, who instigated for killing them, was Hopkins. One Sikh youth- Mewa Singh took the challenge. He spent a lot of fund on bullets to practice perfect aim and prepare himself for the challenge.

Somehow, he entered the house of Hopkins and told him that he would give information about the revolutionaries, if he was given a job in his house. Hopkins believed him. Mewa Singh waited for a proper time. One day Hopkins was shaving before a big mirror. He was sitting. Mewa Singh entered the room with revolver in his hand. Hopkins saw the reflection of Mewa Singh in the mirror and became alert. Mewa Singh lost the chance but played a trick. He kept his revolver on the table and joined his hands before Hopkins. He said- "What happened sir, are you afraid of me and this revolver? Why should I kill you my lord? Do a favour to me. Kill me by this revolver, I will be obliged. As I am working here, my fellow countrymen hate me. I am fed up of my life." He made his face sorrowful and his voice in deep depression. Hopkins believed him and consoled him. After that incident they both became very close.

Mewa Singh became most trustworthy person for Hopkins. On 21st October 1914, the case of Bala Singh was at its last stage. Hopkins was discussing some points with Government lawyer in the court room. Mewa Singh was standing near Hopkins. Mewa Singh shot one bullet directly on the chest of Hopkins and finished his life. The Police arrested Mewa Singh. He did not make any attempt to run away or resist the police.

The case started at court, Mewa Singh said- "Hopkins was a dirty man. He was the cause of fight between brothers and he tried to misguide Sikhs. I don't think it is a sin to kill Hopkins. I have done my duty. If I had failed to kill him, that would have been more painful. For this, Court can give me any punishment, I am happy."

Mewa Singh made his case ease and simple by accepting his crime. He did not take any lawyer for him. He got death sentence. On 11th January 1915, he was hanged. Before hanging, he left a message for all fellow countrymen. He gave it to a local Gurdwara priest who came to visit him in the jail for his last sight. The message was- "I will climb on the hanging board like a baby climbs on the lap of his mother for milk. I will take the hanging rope as a garland of flowers. My last words will be- Waheguru! Waheguru!"

★★★

He grabbed the prey like a lion

The atrocity of British Government made public restless; especially the Wahabi people were very furious. Britishers arrested their popular leaders Ahmedulla and Aamir Khan without any reason. There followers became very upset. Abdullah Wahabi was strong follower of Ahmedulla. He killed Justice Norman with a sharp knife when Norman was climbing the stairs of the court. The incident was of 20th September 1871.

Abdullah was arrested. He had no regrets because his mission was completed. In the court of Calcutta, his case was filed and he was hanged at Calcutta jail.

In 1872, Lord Mayo was the head of Government. He was famous for his atrocities and cruel nature. He made a program to visit Andaman in 1872. For that, cellular jail at Port Blair was prepared to welcome the Lord. Ahmedulla was in the same jail for life imprisonment along with his younger brother.

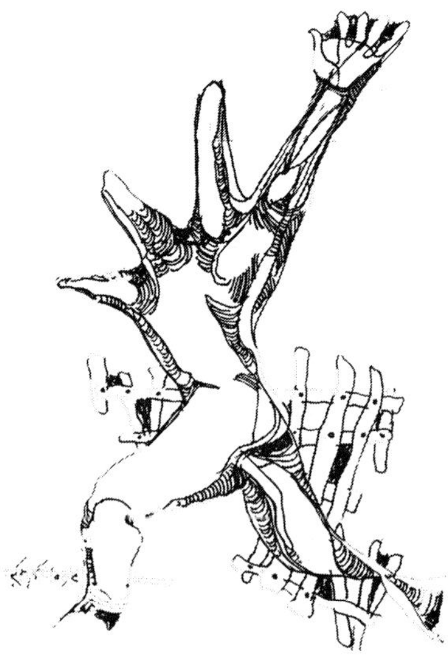

A Wahabi Pathan, Sher Ali from Darra Khyber was also in the same jail. He was a follower of Ahmedulla. He could give his life for his Guru and could take life by the order of his Guru.

Lord Mayo reached Andaman on 8th February 1872. He inspected the jail. After that he was to return India. He was just climbing on ferry boat when suddenly Sher Ali came with a knife and jumped on him. He hit Mayo and he died on the spot. It was the first case of killing of such a big official. Sher Ali took his revenge. Life long imprisonment at cellular jail was more painful than hanging. He preferred death. He took the revenge of the insult to the country. Sher Ali was really a lion of Khyber and he was the brave revolutionary of India. His name is mentioned with the golden words in the history of freedom fight. "Sher-e-Hind Sher Ali zindabad."

★★★

Hindus too loved Maulvi Ahmed Shah

Maulvi Ahmed Shah was a big zamindar in Faizabad district, but he was not like other zamindars. He was a pious and simple man with no ego. He was famous for his good deeds and empathy towards all community and poor people. He was respected equally in the court of the kings and huts of the poor. He was rememberd with honour in every community.

He was neither a Maulvi lost in the religious books nor a person interested in punishing people with tax and making money to lead a lavish life. He was very much interested in the politics of the country and always felt sad that India was gradually being captured by Britishers. Britishers were gaining their place by hook or crook and some of the sons of India were cheating their own country. It was disheartening and he used to talk about this frequently. But, common people were not interested in these matters and Kings and Nawabs were afraid of such talks.

But in 1856, Lord Dalhousie captured Avadh and included it in the company. He arrested Nawab Wajid Ali Shah and sent him to Calcutta. This was untolerable for Ahmed Shah. He understood the fact that in this way Britishers would capture Kings and Nawabs and grab their lands, properties etc. He also understood that the role of public was very important and he started motivating people. He neither went to the Rajas and Nawabs nor to the Muslim gatherings. He went to Hindus and Muslims and asked them to raise arms and fight against English people for the freedom of the motherland. This was the difference between many other leaders of the 'freedom movement of 1857' and Ahmed Shah makes him ever more respected. We wish, if we had some more leaders to be stand with Maulvi Ahmed Shah, we wouldn't have lost the fight of 1857.

Maulvi Ahmed Shah always travelled between Lucknow and Agra to address gathering of thousands of people. He elaborated how the English captured this land and how bad it will be for everyone when they will take complete control of the country. His voice was filled with pain and moved the public emotionally. Maulvi was probably the first to adapt such a form of campaign.

At that time, English had their own spy network that was vigilant about Rajas and Nawabs and hence such propaganda by Maulvi didn't bother them earlier. When they realised its gravity, they tried to arrest him. The police of Avadh revolted and denied to arrest him. Britishers arrested him by army and case was filed against him. He was given a death sentence and till the time of his hanging, he was imprisoned in Faizabad jail.

The arrest of Maulvi Saheb made people agitated. Two platoons of soldiers, some cavalry, and some armoury, which was loyal to English people, revolted. Maulvi Saheb was very popular in Hindus. Subedar Dilip Singh took the first step and imprisoned all English official and declared the freedom of Faizabad from Britishers.

Meanwhile, people reached jail and broke the walls. They released Maulvi Saheb and the public and police declared Maulvi Ahmed Shah as their leader. With that, Faizabad was totally transferred in control of Maulvi Sahib.

After that, the first act of Maulvi Ahmed Shah did something that only he could do. He sent the English people with their family and children to safer place. They were sent by boat; food and necessary items were given to them for their journey. They were given full protection. Maulvi Saheb protected the very same English people who had given him death sentence. It was an example of country's culture. His other friends Raja Mansingh of Shahganj, Sardar Rustom Shah of Saloni and Himmat Singh of Kale Kankad also treated English people in same way.

On the 9th June 1857, Faizabad was declared free from Company's control. It was declared to be under the rule of Wajid Ali Shah. He further made such arrangements so that dacoits and hooligans don't rise up in such freedom, who alway try to take advantage of such opportunity.

★★★

At last, the flag was hoisted

The public of Mumbai were the first to show the agitation against Government Policy. The top leaders of India were taken to some unknown places. It happened suddenly. That was the main reason behind the agitation. Some underground Congress workers formed a working committee and started agitation on mass scale. On the 9th August 1942, curfew was imposed in Mumbai and nearby cities.

Students took out a procession. It was decided that the procession would be dissolved after hoisting Indian flag in Gwaliya Tank Park at Shivaji Park. The procession peacefully proceeded towards the parks but police stopped them on the way. Somehow Aruna Asaf Ali, cheated police and hoisted the flag in the park. There was a peaceful meeting of approximate 10000 people. Police started their brutal actions. Tear gases were used along with lathi charge, and ultimately firing started on the peaceful demonstrators. 5 persons died, 30 injured. Government banned processions and meetings. Approximate 10000 students tried to enter college premises on 10th August but the gates were closed. They peacefully sat in front of the college on road. Gradually people joined them. A huge mass of

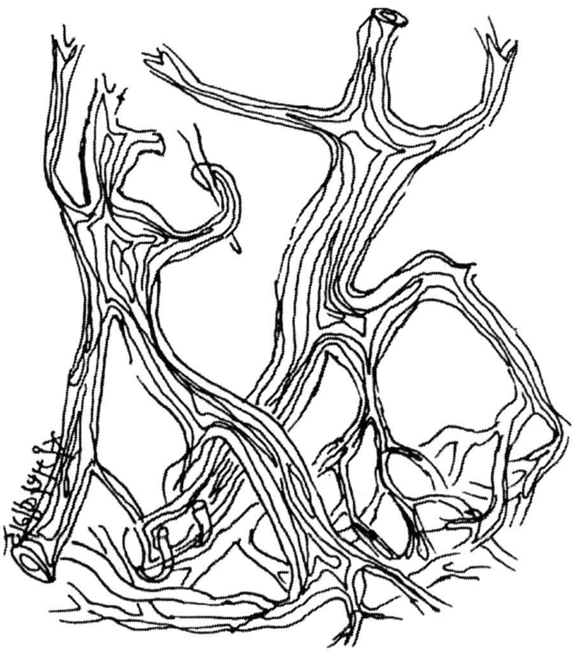

people was mobilized but all were protesting silently. Suddenly police started firing. Firing continued for 15 minutes. 16 people died and many were injured.

At this point, the mob became furious and started destructive activities. B.B.C.I. and G.P.I. Railway Stations were attacked; trams were stopped in the city. There was total Black-Out , because of the destruction of electric wires. It was a big revolt. The revolt was not only in the heart but also came out as words from the people- *Inquilab Zindabad*, *Swatantra Bharat Zindabad*, We will 'Do or Die', *Gandhiji Zindabad*, *Bharat Mata Ki Jay, Bharat Ki Kranti Zindabad* etc. Police had not arranged any ambulance facility. The injured were taken to hospital with the help of local people. So many died at hospital; many even before reaching there. Notification was issued by government again for whiplashing. Many leaders protested but all in vein. Whiplashing started publicly. Young boys were compelled to clean roads, pick garbage, dirt and broken bottles from the streets and lanes. Curfew was imposed. After suffering so much, public lost their patience. They pelted stones on officials. By September, they started throwing bombs. The aggression of public increased with the brutality of police. In October, the agitation was optimum and on 3rd October Madgaon Police Court was burnt.

Actually in Mumbai region, police was prepared to kill people. They were not giving threat or making public go away but they were intentionally firing on the upper side of a person's body.

There were arrests in many places, harassment of common public, looting of property and valuables, intentionally provocating communities against each other; everything done by police. Even Government tried to build communal differences. What ever government had done, they were criticized by their own people. The Advocate General and Government Lawyer of

Mumbai submitted their resignation. The advocate general of Bihar left the job to protest against the atrocities.

★★★

Beastliness of Britishers

Governer General Canning wrote about the inhuman behaviour of English people. He wrote- "English people arrested them and hanged, those who are not guilty but only on the basis of doubt. They looted the villages and burnt all houses, never tried to know who is culprit or who is not. Even they never differentiated man, women and children while punishing them. Now the farming has stopped and India is facing famine like situation." About courts, Mr. Holmes has written "when an army personnel took over the chair of Army Court, he took the oath to hang all the prisoners. The novice soldier used to mock and give painful treatment to the person before hanging and the officers would look the other way with affirmation on their face."

Their behaviour with their own Armymen was not justified or acceptable. On 26th November 1857, they chased about 500 soldiers who ran from Lahore Check Post. They were hungry and had not even water to drink. They got surrounded by soldiers. The soldiers fired on them from all directions. Out of them,

150 injured soldiers jumped into Ravi river and died. Rest injured soldiers were stuffed in a small space; all of them died due to suffocation. Those who were still alive were killed by bullets and thrown into a well which was later recovered. The soldiers fault was that they ran away from Lahore Cantt to Ajnala (Amritsar).

One English man while coming from Ambala to Delhi wrote- "In a while, the sentence to hang was declared for thousands of Hindustanis facing Court Marshall. They were tortured brutely before hanging. Their hairs plucked, body pierced. Even innocent villagers were pierced and forcefully stuffed with Cow meat using javelins."

Mejandi wrote- "There was excessive murders after the victory of Lucknow. There was no difference between soldiers or villagers, black skin was sufficient reason for killing."

Russell wrote in his diary- "Some of the soldiers were still alive but they were brutaly killed. One of them was dragged on sandy field and Britishers pierced their bonnet in his face and body while getting pleasure out of it. Britishers made a small pyre and the man was pushhed in it. The man tried to come out from fire but they again pushed him and stood near with rifle. The live man became ash in few hours." The story of this unknown braveheart brings out the sad state of conditions in India during those days. (1857).

Government ceremony in the middle of corpses

In 1896, the Indians were facing famine. Bal Gangadhar Tilak requested Government to look after the severe problem. He helped famine affected farmers. He took the account of every district and published it in weekly publications "Kesari" and "Maratha".

Famine was persistent and soon the plague spread all over India. Public was in trauma but Government did not bother.

Tilak ji criticized them in his letters. Published all the incidents of famine and plague but the Government was busy with the preparation of Diamond Jubilee function for Queen Victoria. There were uncountable deaths but Government totally ignored those incidents and happily enjoyed the celebration.

At the end, Mr. Rand was deputed to control plague but he was more dangerous than the plague itself. Soldiers vacated the houses in the name of epidemic and burnt them. They sent healthy people to hospitals and some of them were sent to camps. Through these acts the plague was spreading even more. In reality Rand was not at all concerned about the epidemic.

Government gone mad?

Due to all these atrocities of Rand, one youth got furious and killed Rand by shooting him. Police became more brutal. Tilak ji became very angry. In his weekly publication, Kesari, he wrote an article- "Government Gone Mad"? He cursed the Government for its immoral acts. The government was in trouble. Britishers decided to end it and were searching ways to arrest Tilak ji. They knew that till the time Tilak ji is out with public, the Government's existence is in danger.

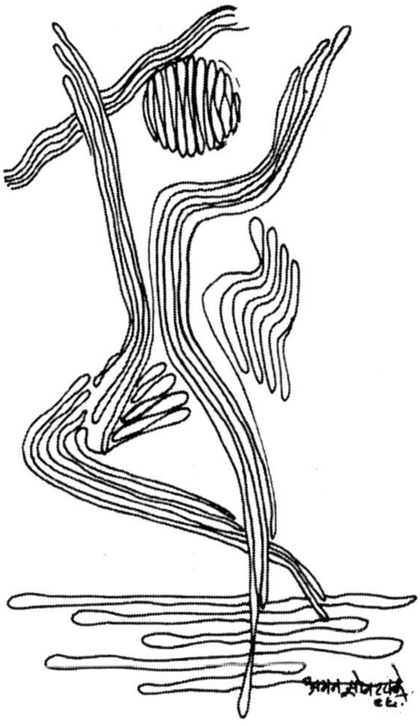

Trading unrest among people, breaking law and instigate people against Government were the charges on Tilak ji. He was arrested and thrown into jail for one and half years.

The lion in a cage

In those days, jail cells were no less than hell. In the dark cell of 13 square feet, no one could sleep while stretching their hands or legs. Rags were full with lice and mosquitoes, bed bugs left prisoners restless without sleep. Sand mixed chapati and dress made of rough heavy cloth. Above all, the officials used to beat the prisoners who were engaged in hard works. Tilak ji used to make ropes and sleeping mats out of coconut fibres. He injured his fingers and palm. The man who was praised by Max Mular for his work Orion, was doing such work which made his fingers bloody. He lost 30 pounds in weight in just four months.

Whenever he got time, he used to write or read. He wrote the famous book "Arctic Home Of The Vedas" while he was in jail.

Fate of country

British divided Bengal. People boycotted the motion there was a fierce agitation. One of the District Magistrates was famous for his brutality. Khudi Ram Bose threw a bomb on him and the person died.

To reduce the unrest among people government became more ruthless. Arvind was arrested with handcuff on his hands and rope on his waist. He was dragged to police station. Only on the suspicion of having explosives, that time, anyone could be arrested and punished with 14 years of imprisonment.

The atrocity of British Government reached its ultimate limit. Tilak ji got perplexed. He wrote an article "Misfortune of Country" in Kesari. Insulted Government and wrote- "It is our misfortune that people of our country are making bombs. But to make bombs and compel youth to throw it, the Government is responsible for creating this situation. Government has made the situation dirty by conducting this injustice to the country."

Britishers were shocked by Tilak ji's direct statement. They again decided to arrest him because he was a great threat to the Government.

Out of country

Due to the article "Misfortune of Country" the charge of treason was put on Tilak ji. On 24th June 1908, he was arrested and deported outside India for six years.

Leadership and scholastic attitude in jail

In Myanmar's Mandalay jail, Tilak ji was residing in a wooden cell with table, chair and book-almirah but he was not allowed to speak to anyone.

One year passed. One of his friends gave him information that if he could agree to the proposals of British Government he could free himself. Tilak ji wrote back to his friend- "Now I am 53 years old. If I live 10 years more, I will get chance to serve my country for 5 years when I come out of this prison. But if I agree to the conditions of the Government, I will die today".

He was given General Imprisonment in place of Rigorous Imprisonment. He was allowed to read and write. *"Geeta*

Rahasya" the famous book was written by him while he was in jail. He spent most of his time in reading and writing. Before the completion of his jail tenure, he collected 400 books. A book named "Self Learning" was written by him and he learnt German and French language.

'Swaraj is our birthright, we will take it at any cost'

Swaraj is our birthright and we will take it at any cost. Japanese are also Asians like us, if they are free then why should we continue slavery? Why are the hands of our motherland handcuffed?"

As the days passed on, the effect of his slogan "Swaraj Is Our Birthright" deeply motivated the minds of the people of India.

To eliminate the British rule from India, he started community based Ganesh Utsav, Shiv Jayanti Utsav. National School Scheme was introduced. He is rememberd as a great patriot, scholar and valiant hero in the history of India's fight for freedom.

❑❑❑